SISTER WENDY'S
NATIVITY

SISTER WENDY'S
NATIVITY

BY

SISTER WENDY BECKETT

For Rachel, Paula, Mary, and all of my beloved sisters at Quidenham

First published in 1998 by HarperCollins*Publishers*
in association with Rose Publishing

Copy editor: Carole McGlynn
Designer: Anthony Cohen
Indexer: Ann Hudson
Illustrations © Ministero per i Beni Culturali e Ambientali, Italy

Cataloging in Publication data for this book is available from the British Library

HarperCollins books may be purchased for educational, business or sales promotional use.

For information please write: Special Markets Department, HarperCollins*Publishers*, Inc.,
10 East 53rd Street, New York NY 10022

ISBN 006 019336 0

Color origination by Colourscan pte, Singapore
Printed and bound in Italy by Rotolito Lombarda SpA

CONTENTS

ABOUT THE MANUSCRIPTS

As a result of a joint program between the Italian Ministry of Culture and the Vatican's Apostolic Library, these precious manuscripts from their extensive collections have been put on exhibition for the first time. Spanning nine centuries, the exquisite images reproduced here illustrate the breadth of style and influence that serve to render these priceless manuscripts so unique.

They include images from late antiquity to the late fifteenth century, created by artists who dedicated themselves to producing art in praise of God, and which illustrate the story of Christ's life from Incarnation to Immortality. Some of the pictures in this book have so far been studied only by scholars in the Vatican and other great Italian libraries.

These manuscripts were created solely to help people pray, to teach them about the truth of their religion, to coax them into thinking more deeply about it and to delight them with their beauty. We trust that you will be equally inspired and delighted.

THE ADORATION OF THE MAGI
Belbelo da Pavia attrib., *Bible of Niccolò III d'Este,*
Vatican City, pre-1434

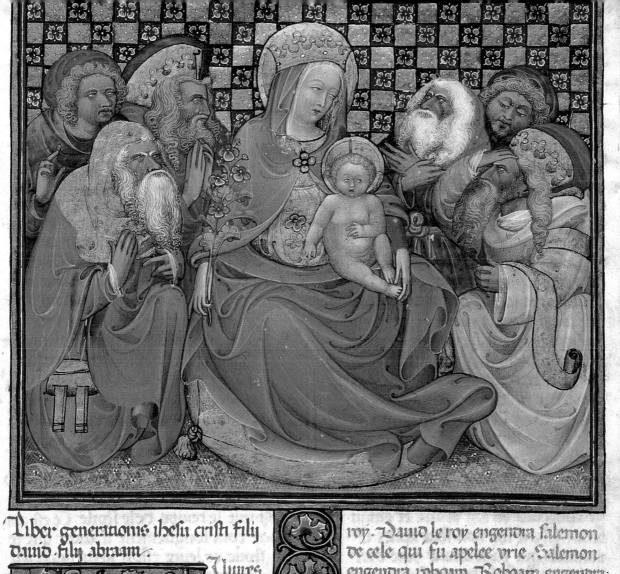

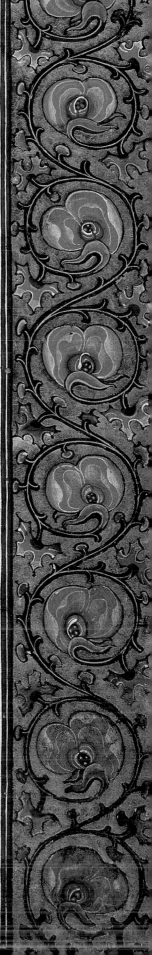

Liber generationis ihesu cristi filij dauid filij abraam.

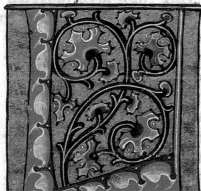

Jluures dela gene ration ie su crist. filz dauid filz abra am. Abia am enge dra yzaac. yzaac en gendra iacob. Jacob engendra iudam et ses freres. Judas engendra phares et aram de thamar. Phares engendra esrom. Esrom engendra aram. Aram engendra aminadab. Aminadab engen dra nason. Nason engendra salemon. Salemon engendra booz de raab Booz de raab engendra obeth et ruth. Obeth engendra iesse. iesse engendra dauid le roy. Dauid le roy engendra salemon de cele qui fu apelee urie. Salemon engendra roboam. Roboam engendra abiam. Abia engendra asa. Asa engen dra iosaphat. Josaphat engendra ioram. Joram engendra oziam. Ozias engen[dra] ioatham. Joatham engendra achaz. A chaz engendra ezechie. Ezechie engen dra manassem. Manasses engendra a mon. Amon engendra iosie. Josie enge[n] dra iechonie et ses freres en la trans migration de babyloine. Cest adire en icel temps que Nabugodonosor en me na les filz ysrael chetis en babyloine Ce fu en icel temps que sechonie qui estoit apelez ioachin fu roys en ieru salem. et empres la transmigration de babyloine sechonie engendra salathiel Salathiel engendra zorobabel. Zoroba bel engendra abiuo. Abiuo engendra elyachym. Elyachim engendra azor.

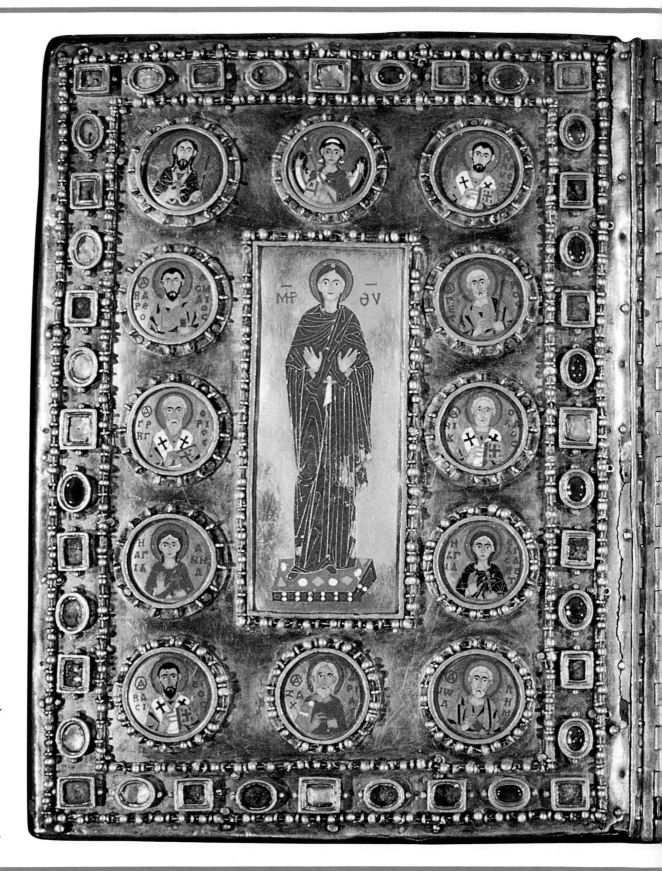

BOOK COVER
Byzantine
(Constantinople)
bookbinding of
Christ Pantokrator
(opposite) and
the Virgin Orans
(right). Silver gilt
on wood, gold
cloisonné enamel,
stones and pearls.
Venice, late 10th–
early 11th Century

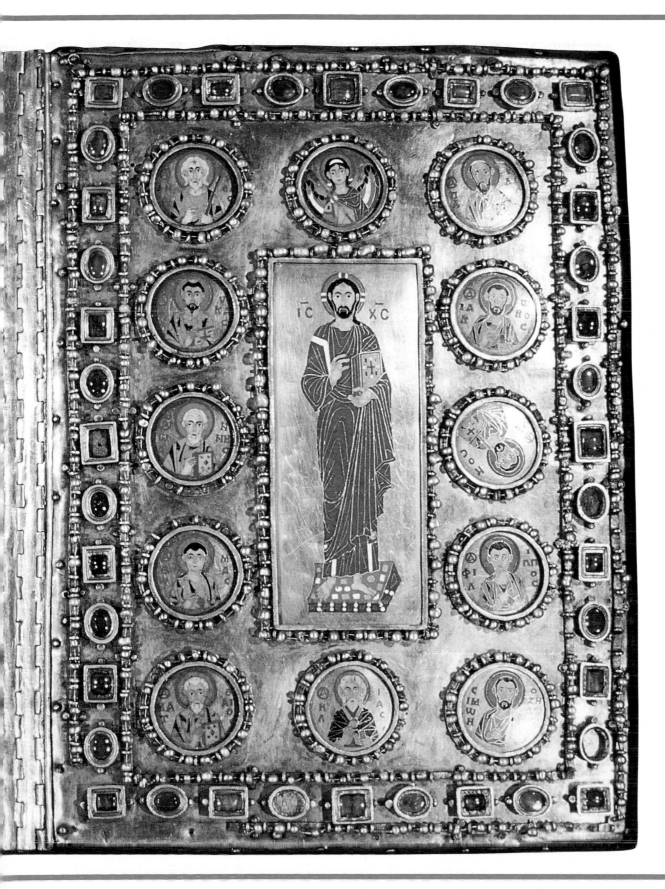

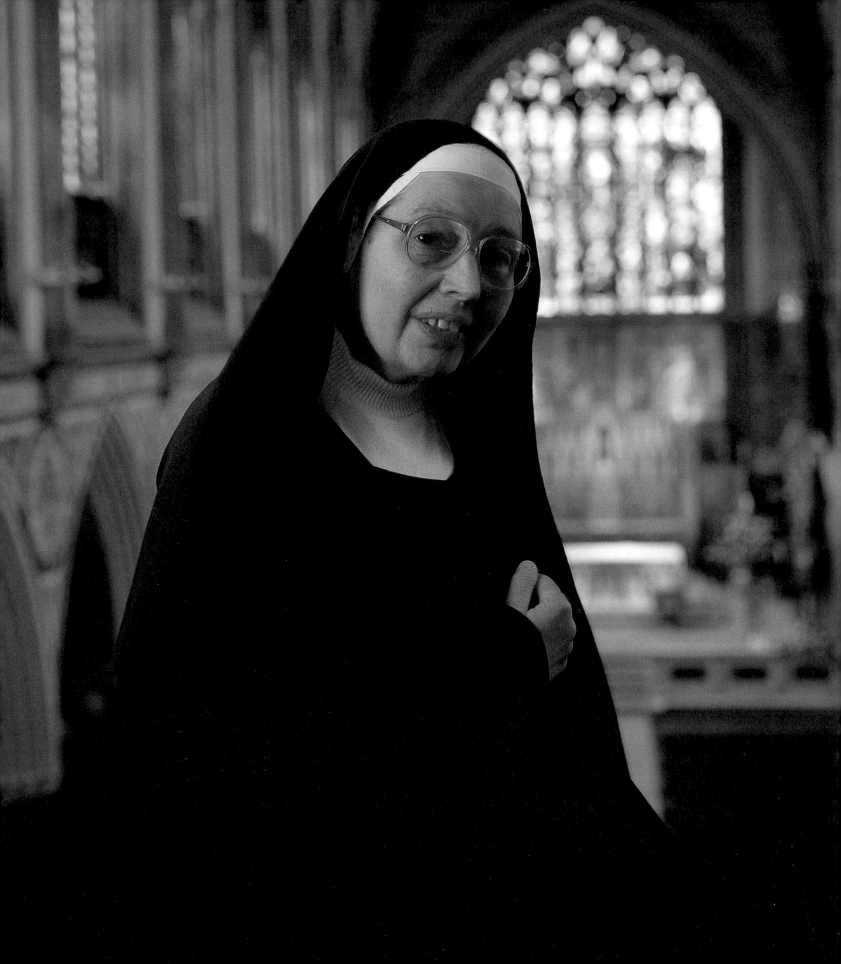

THE STORY BEGINS...

One night, about 2,000 years ago, a momentous event took place. Dorothy Sayers, who did not only write detective stories, described it thus: "Something which was the power of life itself had gone through the world like a thunderbolt and split time into two halves."

The birth of Christ is universally understood as the crucial date in human history. Yet, on the face of it, what exactly happened? In a small town on the outskirts of the Roman Empire, a young mother had given birth to a son, a child of such mystical significance that we still struggle to come to terms with who he was. He was a human child—frail, vulnerable, wailing, totally dependent on his mother for survival. He was also God, that Mystery that is by definition incomprehensible.

"No human being has ever seen God," we are told in Scripture, but Christ could also say that whoever saw him did, in fact, "see God" because He was—incredibly, marvelously—God made man. We shall never understand this. How could such infinite mystery become visible, and so *pathetically* visible? A child is powerless, yet this small human changed the whole nature of our life.

The birth of Christ, proclaiming God's love, set us free in a way so overwhelming and so demanding that we are still baffled by it. The advent of the second millennium is a summons to look more deeply at this birth, and at the events that preceded and followed it, and to seek all over again to accept its glory. Christ came so that we might live life to the full: do we dare?

Dates, on which our history balances itself, hinge on this event: before it, we count backward, from year 1. B.C., meaning Before Christ, takes us back into the prehistoric mists of time. After it, from year 1 A.D., we move forward up to the moment you are reading this book. AD means anno Domini, in the year of the Lord, and that Lord, again, is Christ.

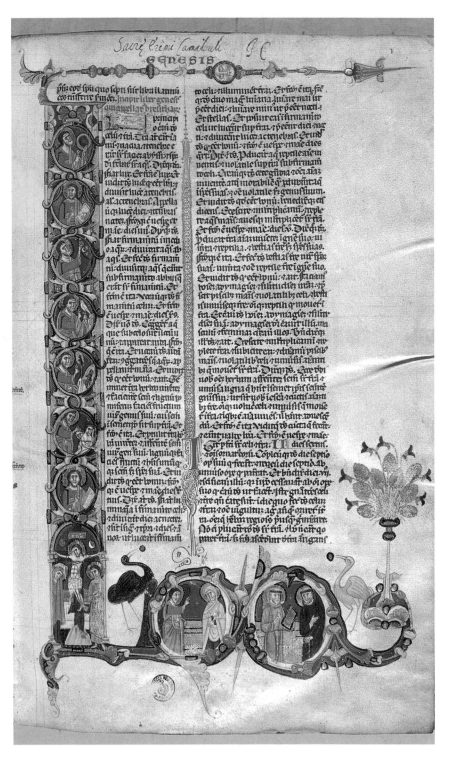

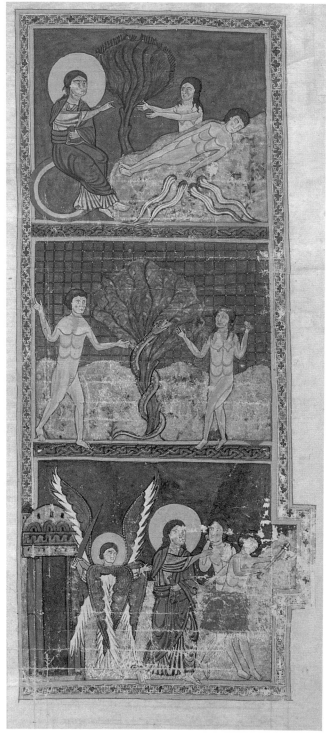

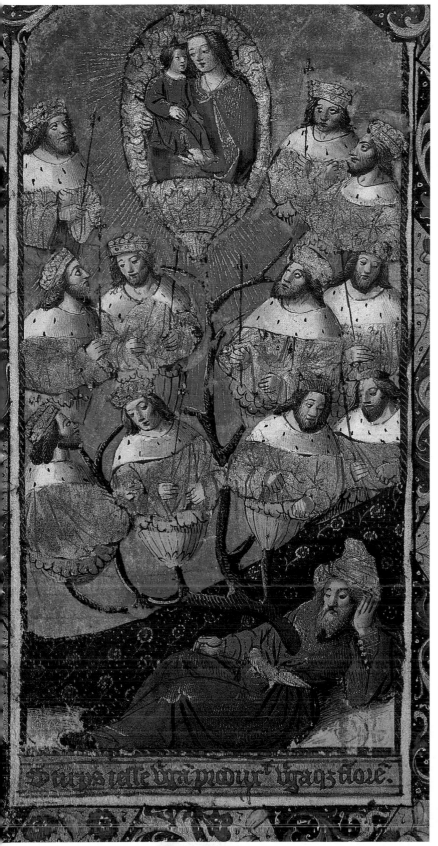

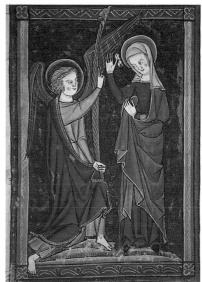

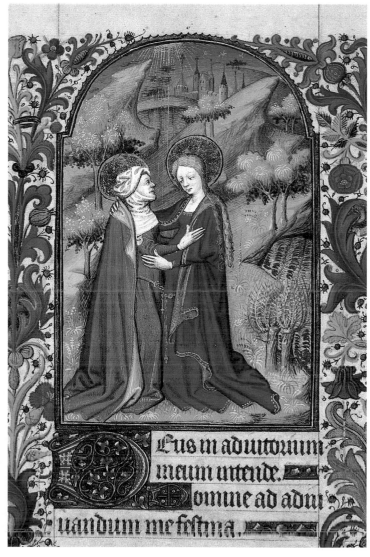

THE CREATION

Saint John begins his gospel with the words "In the beginning," so associating his story with the Old Testament, in which the Book of Genesis opens with the same resounding phrase. How the world began, what human life means, the physics and the metaphysics of existence: these are profound issues that have haunted and intrigued the human imagination throughout time. Theology and science are reconciled in their fascination here, and in so far as both are valid, there need be no contradiction in their findings. Science concentrates on "how" and theology on "why": to this second question Scripture had always given us an unequivocal reply—that the world was created out of love. We all know the story of the six days of active creation, with God "resting" on the seventh, looking with pleasure "at all that He had made"—and concluding that "indeed it was very good." Yet this story is impossible for us to visualize, God being Spirit and the immensity of the universe being beyond our mental grasp.

The artist of this painting accepts from the start that nothing will ever measure up to the inconceivable profundity of the Creation and counts upon our acceptance of the truth of the Genesis story and our sensitivity to its poetic unimaginability. He proceeds to string down his page a "necklace" of time pictures that refer to these mysteries without any attempt at "realism." The first circle shows a brooding God, calling light into being and dividing it from darkness, "the first day" being followed, on the second, by the making of the "vault of heaven" (an image that rather baffles the artist, but he does his best). The third day brings earth with its fruits, and a happy God admiring an apple, then the artist goes adrift and the "apple" changes before our eyes into a putative sun. Sun and moon are created on the fourth day, with God intently communing with a bird (not due to make an appearance until day five). We are back on track for day six, with the creation of human beings amidst an animal world—the goal toward which the Creator had been striving from "the beginning." Yet things are not wholly as they seem: we see God "resting" on the seventh day, then the artist ends his story-beads with something other—the Crucifixion. This, then, was the true meaning of creation. But the end is only apparent, since it is followed, as all know, by the Resurrection.

THE CREATION
Anon., *Bible,* Florence, 13th Century

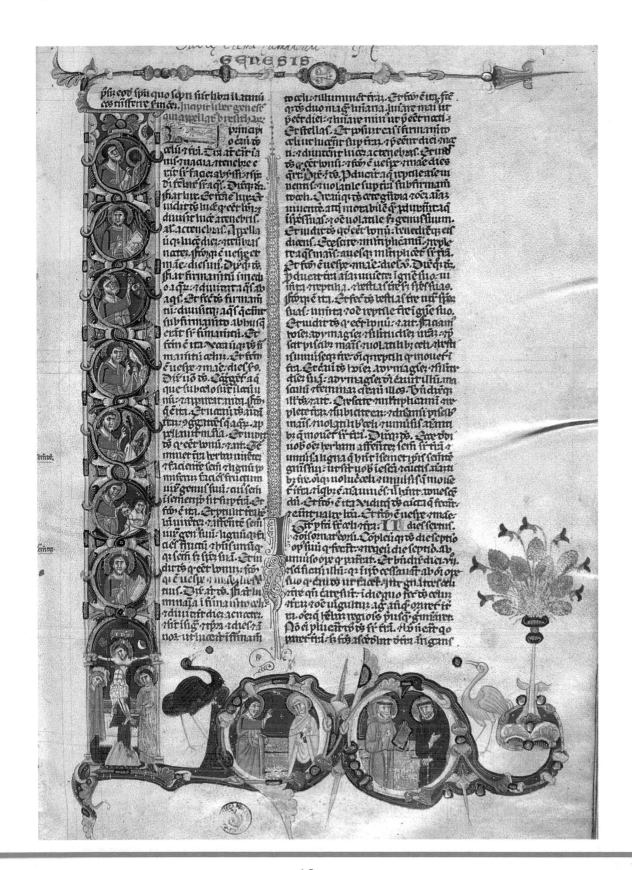

ADAM AND EVE

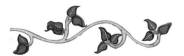

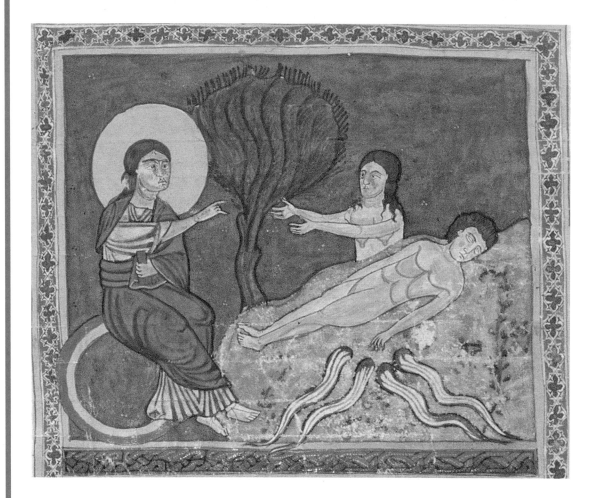

"At the beginning, absolute joy was there for us to embrace— and within ourselves we still feel that joy is 'right' for us."

No theologian doubts that the world was created "for" Christ: He was its fulfillment and gave it its meaning. What remains a matter of reverent speculation, though, was whether the way Christ's life unfolded—his birth and his terrible death, and then the Resurrection—was intended from the beginning or came about only because of Adam and Eve, our first parents. God had set them in Paradise, as is clearly shown in this

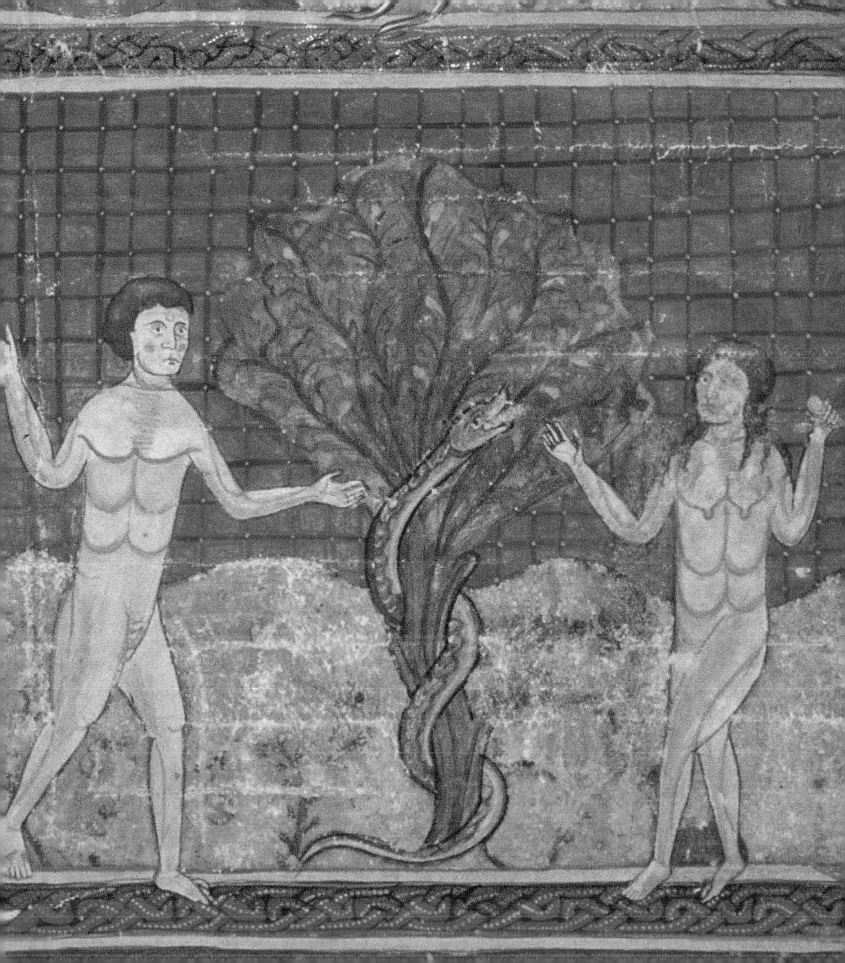

"Even here, there is a hint of the redemption to come, of a future birth—and redeeming death."

painting. The first picture shows God reclining on the sun and summoning Eve into being to partner a sleeping Adam; beneath him, on the grassy bank, the four rivers of Paradise gush out to the corners of the earth.

Except for the birth of Christ, the Fall is the the most important event in human history. The Fall itself is pure tragedy, but God in his goodness turns this disaster into a reason to love him. Everything depicted by this rather faltering artistic hand has meaning only in relation to what is to come: the Birth. Mary will be the new Eve, as wise as her predecessor was foolish, as thoughtful as our first mother was thoughtless, as clothed in the goodness of God as Eve is naked. Nothing impresses upon us the absolute need of our Saviour more than the images of our first parents and their deliberate refusal to obey. At the beginning, absolute joy was there for us to embrace—and within ourselves we still feel that joy is "right" for us. We resent sorrow, and though we are all over familiar with it, it never feels anything but alien. Joy we accept as our natural homeland, though it was a homeland we soon lost.

The Bible tells of temptation, of a refusal to obey God, of Eve's deliberate choice of rebellion. In this second painting the serpent of deceit offers Eve the apple of sin, showing both Eve and her partner eager for the new experience; the significance is clear enough.

The artist is not very good on anatomy, as

pages 16, 17 and opposite:
ADAM AND EVE AND THE GARDEN OF EDEN
Anon., *Bible*, Florence, 12th Century

the third picture proves—and he may have been grateful that from now on a red kilt would modestly shroud humanity's genitals—but there unmistakably are Adam, holding a gardening tool (the Fall brought with it the need to work), and Eve turning sadly back toward a God who is saying farewell. The gate of Paradise stands open, but the way in is barred by a resolute angel, the only angry figure in the picture.

There is a sad irony in the foolish alacrity with which Adam and Eve rush to their doom. Their body language expresses only compliance—they seem not even to pause to think and consider the serpent's offer. These two naked simpletons brought us into a world of pain and labor, so the artist suggests, and our flowering tree of life was strangled by the serpentine embrace of the enemy.

God is making promises—He will send his Son, the exile will not be eternal—but the angel, the outline of his sharp features echoed by the rigidly held sword, seems hostile. Then we notice that his arms are outspread in the shape of a cross. Even here, there is a hint of the redemption to come, of a future birth—and redeeming death.

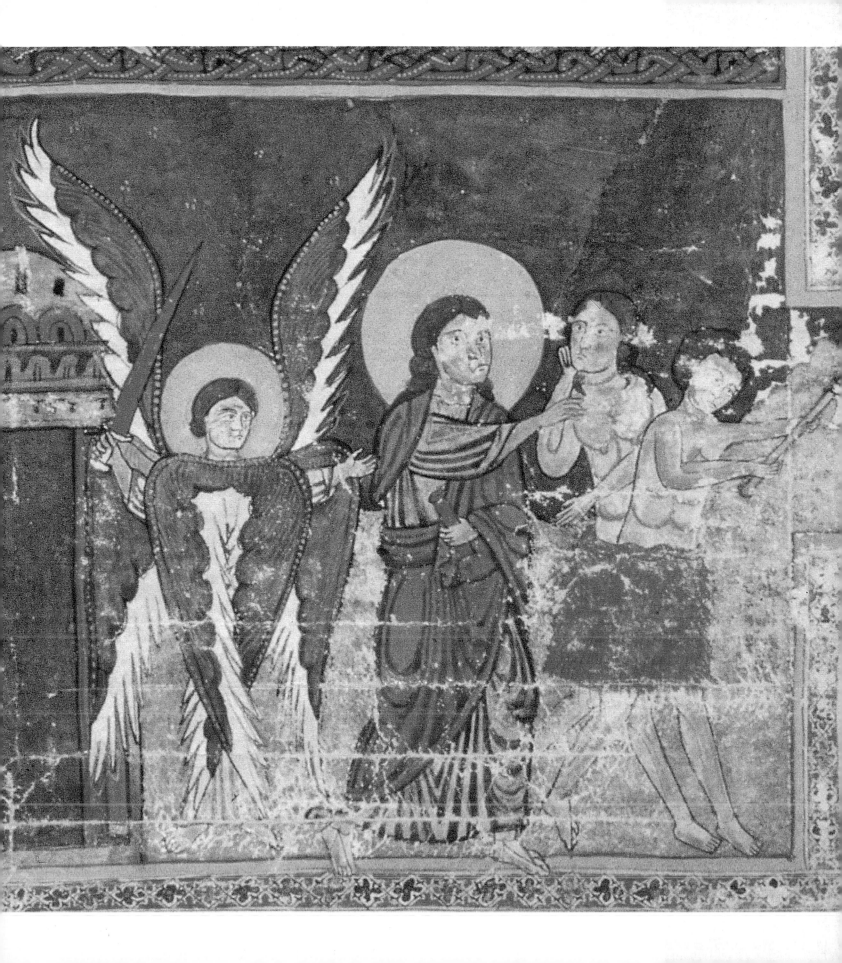

THE TREE
OF JESSE

"In the medieval imagination, the ancestry of Christ centered on the person of Jesse, the sheep farmer of Bethlehem, with seven sons and a young, unconsidered eighth, David."

For the Christian, everything in the Old Testament foreshadows the events in the New. The Bible stories were true and yet also symbolic, since their full meaning was revealed only in Jesus.

When Saint Matthew describes Jesus entering Jerusalem amidst cries of popular acclamation, the crowd hails him as "son of David," because this most famous of historical Jewish kings was traditionally held to be the ancestor of the Messiah-to-come. David was the greatest of all men and women on Christ's family tree, but there were many others (Saint Luke takes it all the way back to Adam, but Saint Matthew is modestly content to start his genealogy at Abraham). In the medieval imagination, Christ's ancestry centered on the person of Jesse, the sheep farmer of Bethlehem, with seven sons and a young, unconsidered eighth, David. It was David, of course, who was to be "the ancestor," despite his chequered career, in which murder and adultery coexist with courage, imagination, and a charismatic lovability that is unforgettable. In picture after picture, artists portrayed Jesse as dreaming of the family tree that would arise from his body,

bearing the long line of kings of Israel and culminating in Mary and her son, Jesus.

The sleeping Jesse in this painting has a look of complacent satisfaction, with all his descendants crowned, ermine-draped, golden and glorious. This is an abbreviated "tree," simply indicating the passage of generations, but the uniform virtue of the sons of Jesse is hardly borne out by biblical records. David's son, Solomon, however famous for his wisdom, came sadly adrift with his numerous wives, and then there was Tamar the harlot and Ruth the non-Jew.

The ancestry of Jesus is as richly diverse as that of anyone, and as interesting. But here the interest is not in the character of the long line of individuals that make up the tree, only in the original "ancestor" (insofar as anyone can be that), Jesse, and his final fruit, shown as a gleaming globe of gold with mother and child at its center. The artist depicts the immediate forebears as reverently conscious of their blessedness while the others, like the rest of us, are sublimely unaware of what lies ahead.

THE GENEALOGY OF JESUS
Anon., *The Blessed Virgin Mary's Book of Hours*, Naples, 15th Century

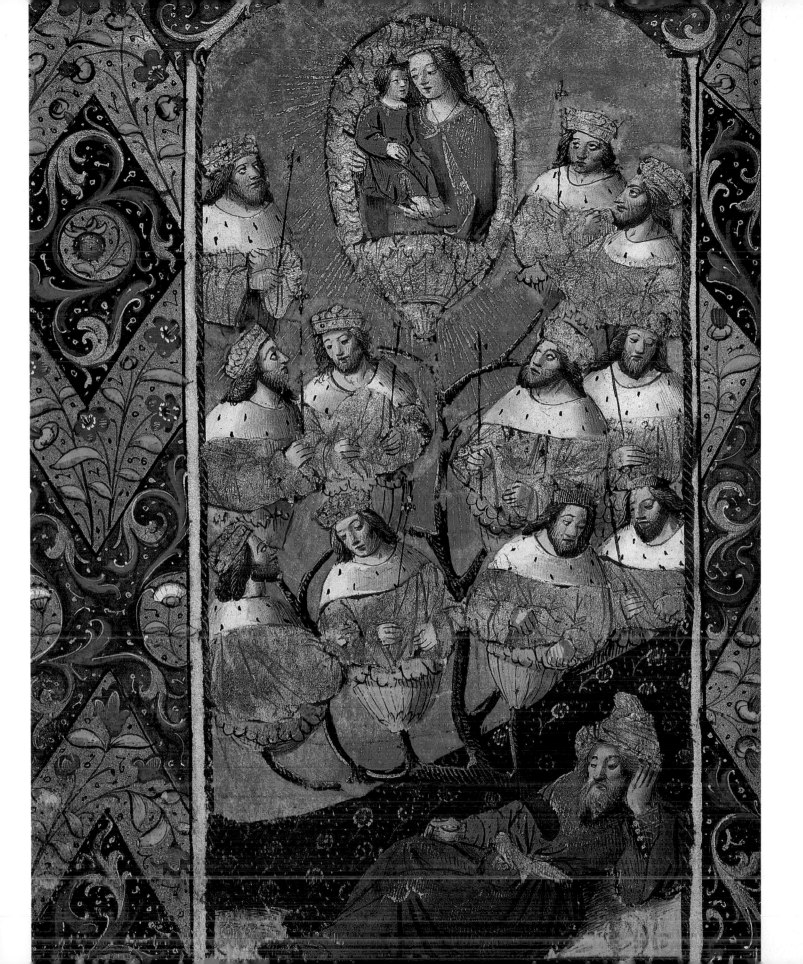

THE ANNUNCIATION

"The problem, expressed by the nervous and protective clutching of her cloak, is that she cannot have a child, as she is not yet married."

While Jesse and his descendants were acknowledged as remote forerunners of Christ, Adam, that ultimate progenitor, was lost in the mists of prehistory. But Christ's *immediate* ancestor was that slender figure around whom so many legends were to wreathe their poetry, the Virgin Mary. We know from Saint Luke that she was a girl living in Nazareth (not even mentioned in the Old Testament among the biblical cities of note) and that she had become engaged to a man called Joseph, who was descended from David. We are told nothing of her own family and given little direct insight into what she was like, this young woman chosen by God to be the mother of His incarnate Son.

The artist concentrates on this unique historical significance, taking Mary and the angel out of real space and setting them upon a blue-green base with what once must have been a burnished gold background, reminiscent more of heaven than of earth. The base is the green of the fields, but neither Mary nor the angel really belong there. The angel, Gabriel, kneels in awe to announce her calling, his face bright with the joy of the encounter. He is often shown holding a lily, in honor of Mary's virginal purity, and it may well be that what the artist here depicts is his idea of an Oriental version of this. The long stalk serves to divide the picture into two halves, so that Mary is isolated in the moment of her acceptance.

The problem, expressed by the nervous and protective clutching of her cloak, is that she cannot have a child, as she is not yet married. Gabriel's solution is that this is to be a supernatural birth. The child will be "holy, the Son of God." The dialogue, expressing astonishment and fear, seems to have already taken place. Mary holds aloft an astonished hand, but is bowing her head submissively. The reader can almost hear those moving words: "I am the handmaid of the Lord: Be it done to me according to your word." The meaning of the message is becoming clear to her, as far as something so mysterious can ever be clear. Her face is set, in an expression half-smiling, half-anxious. But the angel is all exultant happiness.

THE ANNUNCIATION
Anon., *Psalter*, Venice, 1270–80

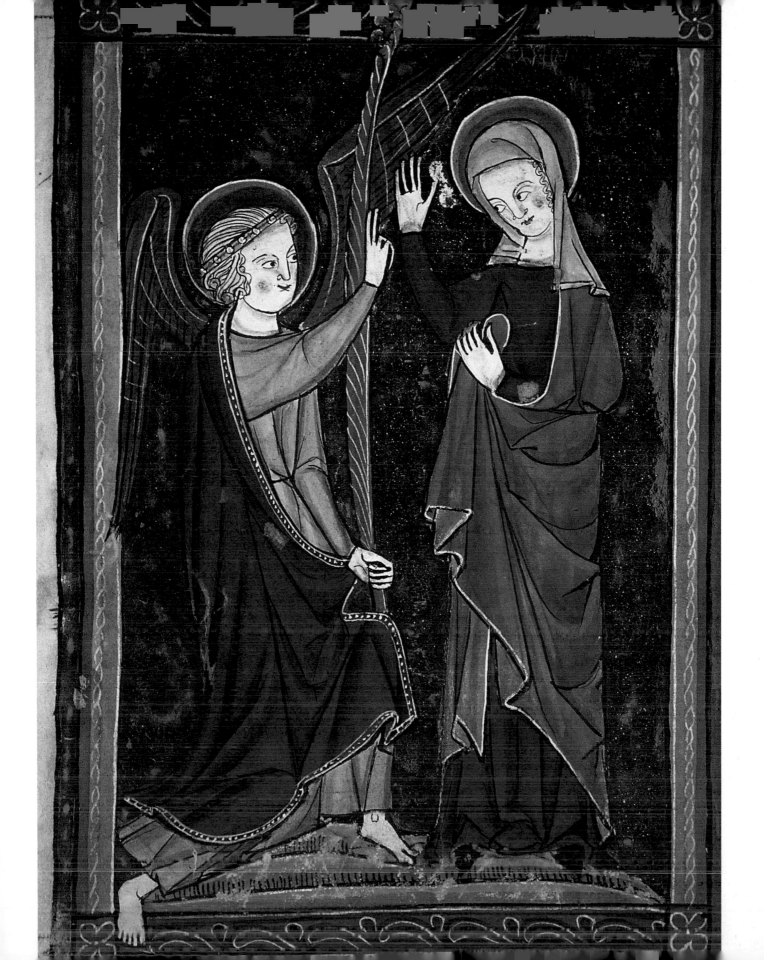

THE ANNUNCIATION (II)

This Annunciation, in its lovely border of blue and gold tendrils, is less concerned with the interaction between angel and woman and more eager to make the announcement seem "real" to us. The artist provides a complete setting, and a grand one at that. (Rational argument is not the issue here, but one could make the point that Scripture tells us Gabriel found Mary alone, suggesting that she was not from a family so poor that privacy was impossible for her.) The affections of the church urged both the artists and those who commissioned them to boost Mary's status: even if logic told them that there were, in fact, no Jewish princesses in Nazareth, merely some highly dubious ladies in Herod's palace in Jerusalem, they nevertheless liked to see her portrayed in circumstances of the utmost splendor. This little Mary, her fair head gleaming above clasped hands, kneels on a floor of exotic tiles, while Gothic magnificence towers around her. Both she and the angel

are, quite literally, too great for their space. The angel could never pass up the winding stair to his left, and nor could Mary. What this picture depicts so well is the immediacy of Mary's response to God. The admonitory finger tells us that Gabriel has hardly finished his speech, but already Mary is irradiated by a shaft of spiritual light, as God the Father breathes on her and she immediately becomes pregnant. Artists often show the Dove of the Holy Spirit luminous in this light, and a careful examination of this picture will reveal the white outline of his presence here, almost equidistant between the Father (heaven) and the Virgin (earth). This was the great and central meaning of the Incarnation, the linking of these two opposites, one all-powerful and holy, the other, as we know only too well, powerless and not holy in the least. So power and weakness join in Mary, and become redemptive in her Son.

THE ANNUNCIATION
Anon., *The Office of the Blessed Virgin Mary*, **Florence, 1407–8**

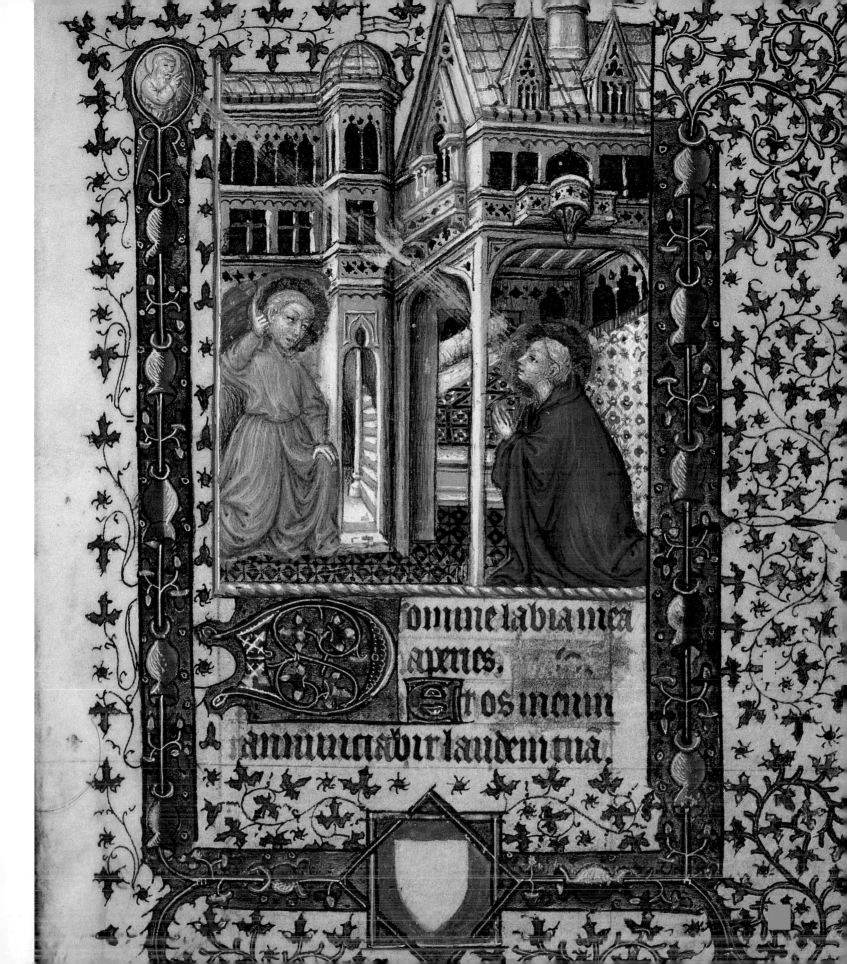

omine labia mea
apenes.
Et os meum
annunciabit laudem tuã.

THE VISITATION

Mary did not ask for any sign from the angel: she believed with pure faith. But she was given what she had not requested, and the sign was one that paralleled her own miracle, but at a distance.

Her cousin Elizabeth had grown old without a child, thought then to be a sign of God's displeasure, and an abiding grief for the deprived couple. But Elizabeth is already six months pregnant, the angel tells Mary (although, tactfully, he chooses not to tell her that her cousin's husband, Zachariah, has been unable to believe his own angelic message, and has been struck dumb for a time in consequence).

"Mary arose with haste," we are told, and set out undaunted into the hill country of Judah to visit her cousin. Saint Luke says they met in Zachariah's house, but for this artist, it is more appropriate to show them embracing in a wide and fertile landscape. It is not a safe world: the surrounding hills look like frozen rockets, sharp and hostile. But at the spot where the two women meet they seem to bring with them, or to call into being by their presence, trees and

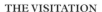

grasses. City towers pierce the skies in the far distance, while they stand motionless under the soft brightness of a country sun. Neither smiles: the encounter is too solemn for gaiety.

Mary knows that Elizabeth's pregnancy is miraculous, and Elizabeth knows Mary bears within her the Salvation of the world. She hails her "Blessed among women, and blessed is the fruit of your womb." The wombs touch, the unborn John the Baptist leaps with joy and his mother cries at the nearness of the unborn Jesus. This is a picture whose deepest truth is invisible.

The artist cannot portray the moment the babies encounter each other: we only know of it through Elizabeth's ecstatic report of the leap she feels within her.

THE VISITATION
Jacobus Coen attrib., *The Blessed Virgin Mary's Book of Hours*, **Naples, 15th Century**

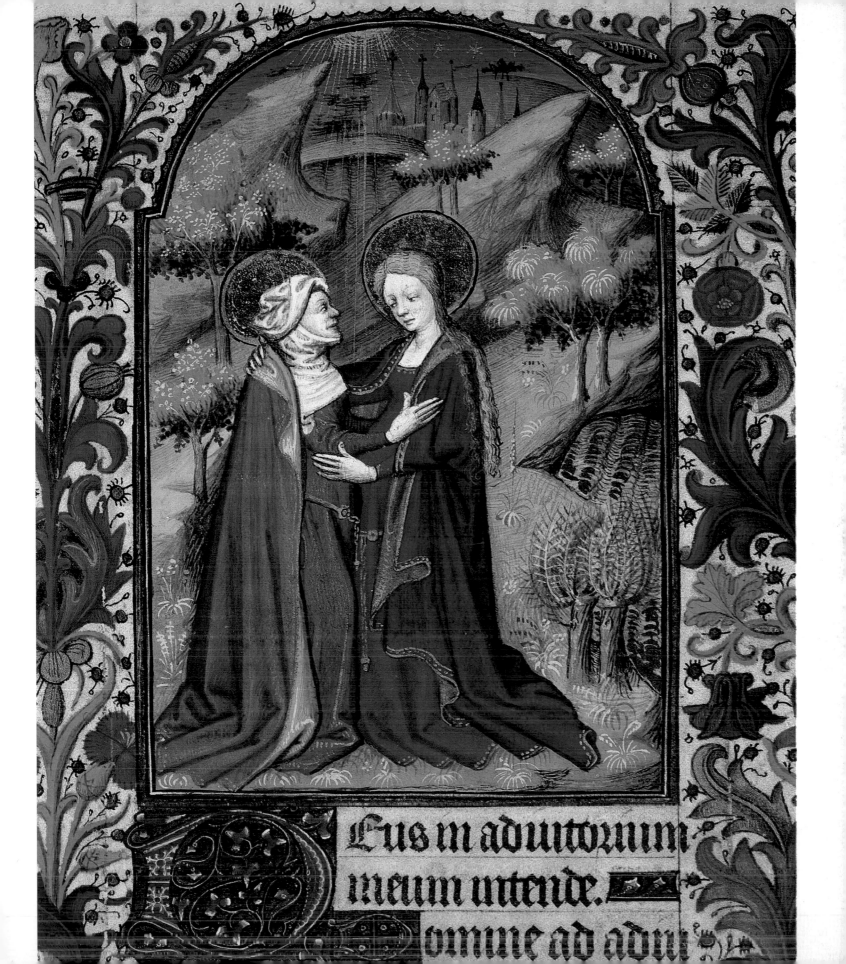

Eus in adiutorium
meum intende.

Domine ad adui

THE VISITATION (II)

The splendid pillared frame in this picture might persuade us that this artist is attempting biblical accuracy and that this is the house of Zachariah, much upgraded from a village cottage. But no: once again the cousins are meeting in the open air, and only the battlemented pile behind shows that one of them, at least, has not ventured far from "home." These are surely symbolic towers, suggesting the inner security of one who trusts in God. Elizabeth and Mary both chant hymns of joy when they meet, and Elizabeth's ends with that great affirmation of the power of faith: "Blessed is she who believed that the promise made her by the Lord would be fulfilled."

We get what we believe in, as Jesus himself would later tell his disciples. If we expect great things from God, we will receive them, but disbelief makes this impossible.

The emphasis in this picture is on the faces, Elizabeth's awed, almost afraid, tremulous with the wonder of God's goodness, but showing her years. Mary looks almost pitifully young, a gentle child who has given herself to God to "glorify the Lord," whose "spirit rejoices in

THE MAGNIFICAT
Mary's song of praise, the Magnificat, has been sung every day in churches all over the world. The song marvels at the ways of God, who alone can "fill the starving with good things and send the rich away empty."

God my Saviour." With objective humility she is well aware that "all generations" will call her "blessed," solely because God has chosen her, of his own will. Mary's downward glance at her ripening womb speaks of her growing understanding of God's power, and of its unearthly nature.

The proud and the princely are invincible in worldly terms, but not in the eyes of God. They are powerless against death and disease, and any hardness of heart will be mercilessly revealed on the Day of Judgment. Yet God's apparent mercilessness is in fact an act of supreme mercy: it is the essential truth. For the mighty to be shown their own reality may be painfully subversive, but therein ultimately lies their salvation.

THE VISITATION
Anon., *The Office of the Blessed Virgin Mary,*
Florence, pre-1468

"If we expect great things from God, we will receive them, but disbelief makes this impossible."

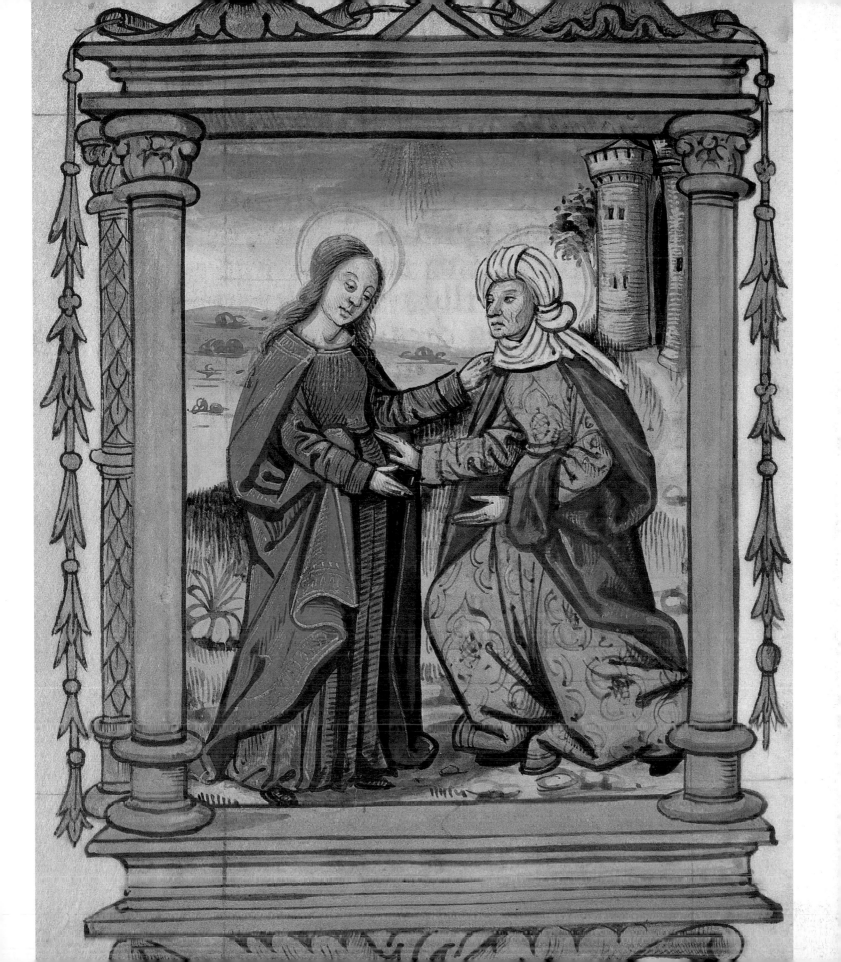

JOSEPH'S DREAM

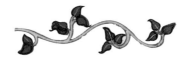

Mary's perplexity about a virginal pregnancy was not argued away by Gabriel but simply challenged: this is God's business, and He will overshadow you. It would seem, from Saint Matthew's account of the Visitation, that Mary regarded this promise as inherently private, and waited trustfully for God to explain things to her betrothed. Mary, we should remember, was not simply an unmarried woman, she was formally engaged to "a just man" called Joseph, and engagement under Jewish law implied a precontractual marriage. The birth of Christ can seem utterly removed from the everyday reality of our own life, elevated into a sacred sphere where all is peace and joy. Not so: Mary is living in a real world, though in her innocence she may not have appreciated its full dimensions. And Joseph, as an adult male, presumably in love with his young betrothed, was shaken to the core to find her visibly pregnant. We can well imagine the tumult of emotions this discovery invoked. There was the pain of personal rejection, knowing as he did that he was not the father of the coming child. Even more wounding must have been a sense of having misread Mary's character: she had

seemed—still seemed, presumably—so true and good, yet she had not only deceived and cheated him, but was continuing to do so.

There is no suggestion that Mary ever sought to release Joseph from his promise, although Joseph wrestled with the problem of how to break the engagement without bringing her into disrepute. Mary's trust in God to enlighten her beloved was magnificently vindicated. Joseph is not visited by an angelic vision, but he has that next best thing, a dream. In the dream, the angel of the Lord tells him emphatically that "what she has conceived is through the Holy Spirit": Mary and Jesus need Joseph's protection, and to give this is his hard and lonely vocation. This wonderful image shows the angel shooting toward Joseph like a projectile from heaven: a spiritual rocket is about to land on his anxious slumbers, and his rational world will deconstruct. The angel is all tense dynamite, while Joseph suffers in a nightmarish sleep: the impact is with us still. This "dream" would overturn all his certainties and make possible the survival of mother and son. It is a reassuring dream, emotionally, but the repercussions are immense.

JOSEPH'S DREAM
Anon., *Concerning the Virginity of Mary*, Florence, 10th Century

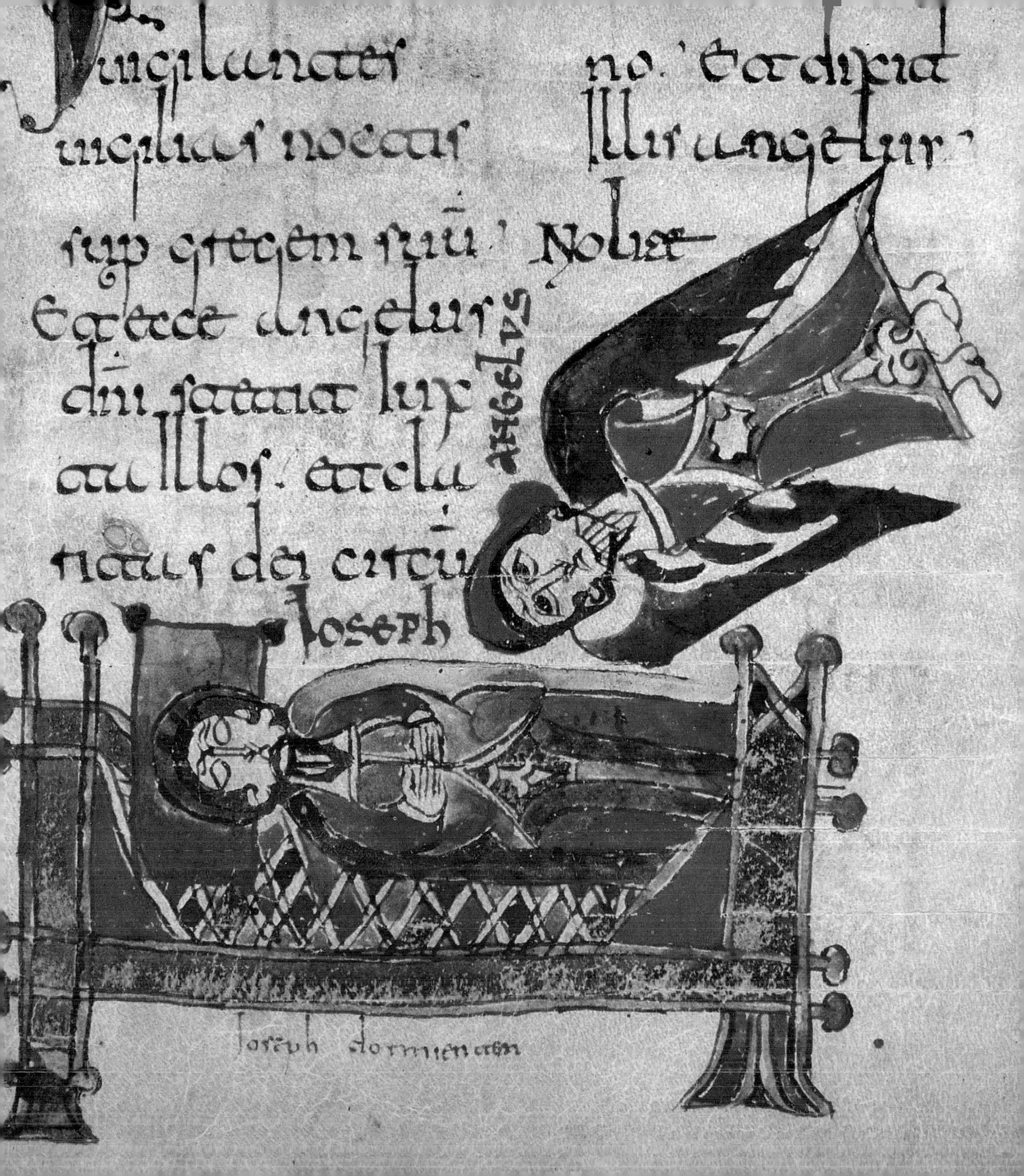

Incipit uaciat
uigilias noccas
sup gregem suu·
et ecce angelus
dni sactuta lux
ca illos· et clu
ticas dei circu

no· et dixit
illir angelur
Nolit

ANGELVS

Ioseph

ioseph dormientem

THE HOLY BIRTH

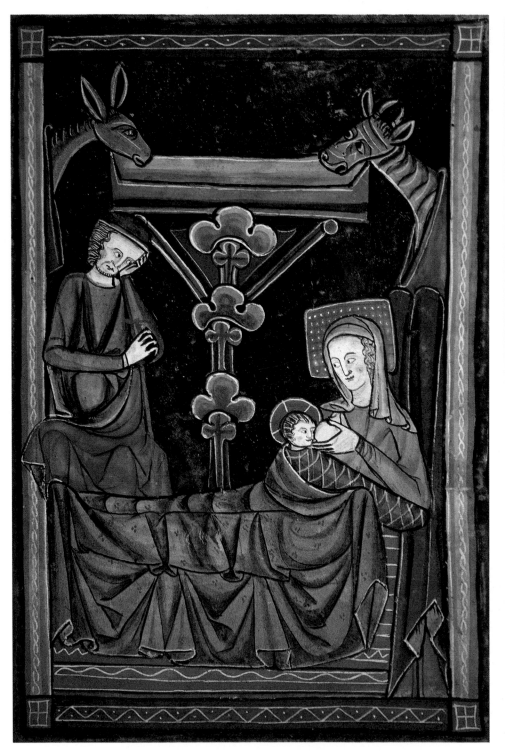

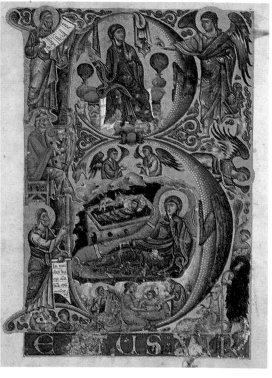

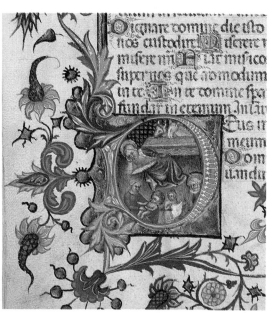

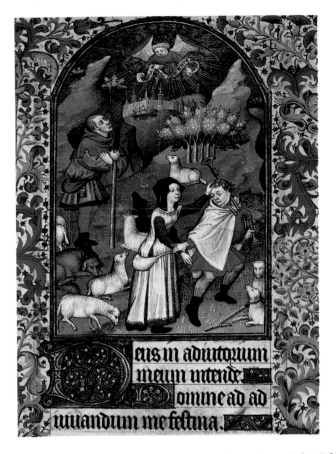

Salue regina mîricordic. uita dulc
do tertiam offitium. Versus

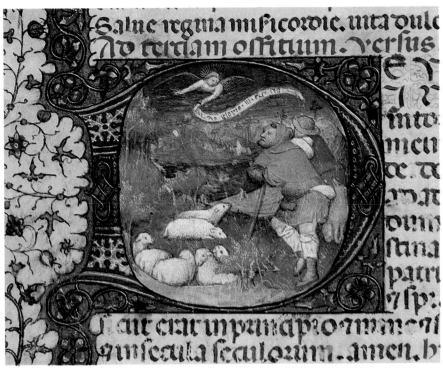

eus in adiutorium
meum intende.
omine ad ad
iuuandum me festina.

it erat in principio nunc 7
in secula seculorum. amen. h

e mira. Srecuando la responsione in sonno
che illi non coueseno tornare ad herodes. e leua
rose retornono per altra uia in le so contrade.

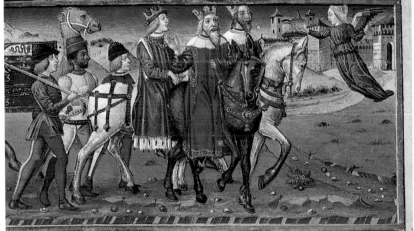

Questo sie lo euangelio como lo angelo aparse
in sonno a ioseph dicando debie fugire in egipto
con lo fantolino e con santa maria per che herodes
cercha de farlo ocidere lo fantolino.

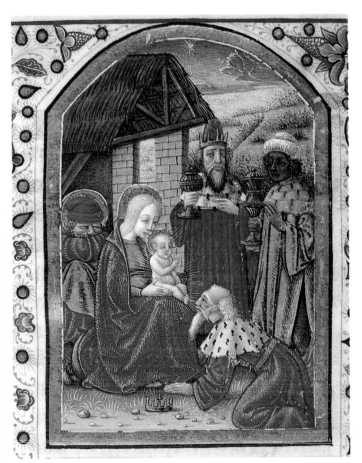

THE NATIVITY

The image of the nativity, the birth of Christ, must be the most familiar in Western art. Even those who never go to art galleries or read art books get Christmas cards. In fact, the image is probably overfamiliar to us, and it helps to see it afresh, as in this little painting, nestling into the curves of a capital D, which sets out very simply and with a bright clarity the essence of the Nativity "story." Here we see the father, mother and newborn child, in neither a hospital nor a home, but roughing it in the crude, open stable with the attendant animals. This lovely image cannot be said to be great art in the strictest sense—its richness lies in the charm of its simplicity.

The little Jesus is the center: He is radiantly white, and golden rays gleam out from his body in all directions. He is curiously alone: his mother stays a little removed, lost in prayer, though the child reaches out to her, while his stepfather, Joseph, is hulking supportively in the background. Lassoed in the pink-and-white curlicues of the large D, the small family, not to mention the awed and interested ox and ass, seem isolated in a silent beatitude. Stars shine in a brilliant sky, grass glows with the richest of greens, and trees burst from the earth. They are enclosed in a private world, where all colors are pure and beautiful, where all presences are protective, and where even the beasts seem aware of love.

The painter feels a need to impress this upon us with strong gestures: this is how he thinks it was, and this is what he expects us to know, too. Unfortunately, what we know is that this is rather how we would like it to have been. But the truth is that Jesus was born into the real world, and so the wonder of his birth must be framed by what came before and by what happened after it.

THE NATIVITY
Jacobus Coen attrib., *The Office of the Blessed Virgin Mary*, Turin, 15th Century

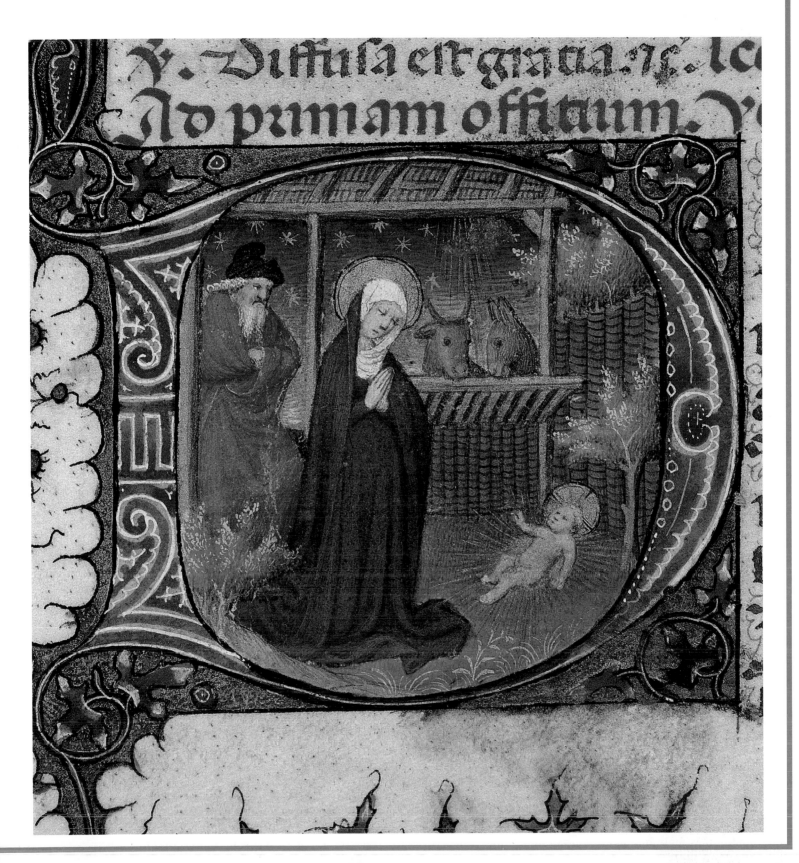

THE NATIVITY (II)

The major artist who painted this miniature has a great sense of drama. Color is of secondary importance to him, crucial only insofar as it highlights the narrative, the personal interactions, the profoundly religious nature of the scene. Here Joseph is still apprehensive, and very much an outsider. The strange object in his hands is probably a lily, a symbol that he is not the physical father of the newborn child. Mary, wonderfully composed of graphic lines and pleats, is portrayed as a real mother. She has swaddled her child, she holds him and suckles him. Her face expresses only a tentative happiness, tense and exhausted, as is common with firstborn children. The little Jesus is shown as an ordinary baby, tight within his wrappings, and gazing at his mother's full breast with mild surprise. The artist here is not concerned with making any attempt at realism. He likes patterning and must have taken much pleasure in painting the elaborately decorated feeding trough that rises from Mary's bed. The bemused ox and ass eye each other across it, as baffled as humankind has been ever since.

What this picture, minimal in its narrative, but immensely powerful in its conviction, makes clear is that what happened in the stable at Bethlehem is not subject to human explanation. The ox and the ass are, as it were, our surrogates—present, impressed, but fundamentally uncomprehending. Mary and Joseph do not understand either, and Saint Luke is to add that "Mary pondered all these things in her heart." What it all meant would reveal itself later, after Christ's death and resurrection, and then through the ages of Christian thought and prayer. We are still at a loss, just like the animals in the stable; like them, we can see the outline of its meaning—and this artist is particularly good with outlines.

But beyond that? Like Mary and nervous Joseph, we believe that this holy birth has transformed our lives, not only revealing the love of God, unearned and total, but also showing us the potential of our own enfeebled selves. It is beyond us to take all of this in—but we *do* believe.

THE NATIVITY
Anon., *Psalter*, Venice, 1270–80

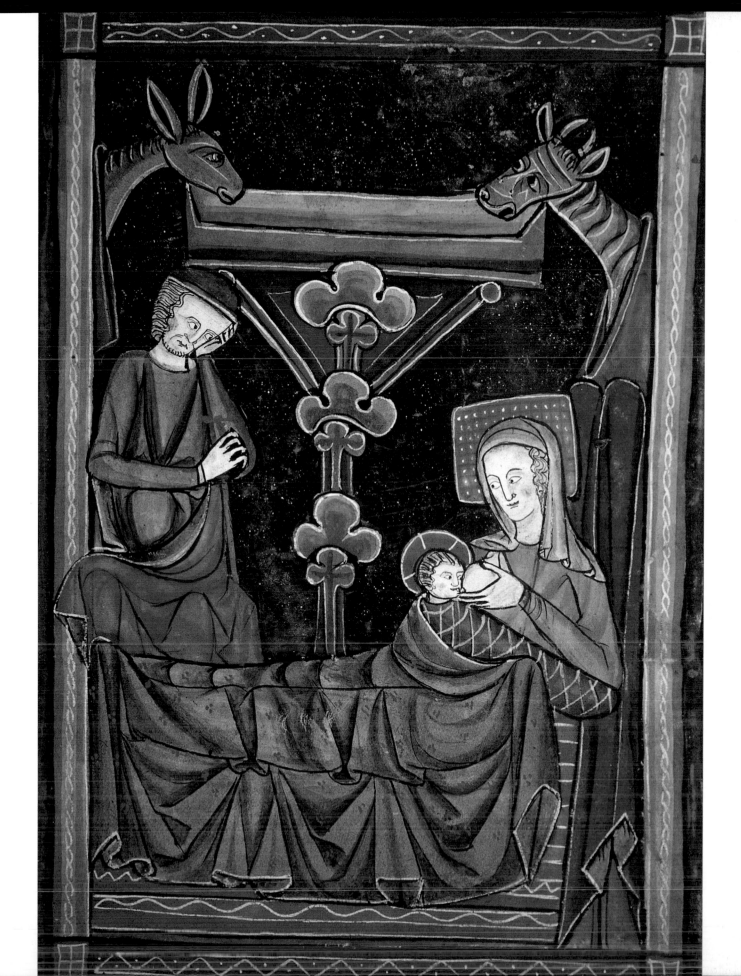

THE NATIVITY (III)

"...*God is not punitive in his actions, and this is something His Son would spell out again and again. Perhaps the artist was aware of this.*"

This tiny picture, with the D of 'deus' expanded to take an insertion, is one of the few illuminated manuscripts to show a midwife.

This was a legend, fruit of that intense curiosity of the early church to know more than the gospels told them. The gospels were not meant to be "biographies." They never describe Jesus, for example: how we would love to know what He looked like! They are concerned only with his message—with what he was and what this meant for us—and the attractions of holy gossip seem not so much to have been resisted as not to have presented any temptation at all.

The story of the midwives is typical of the desire of later generations to enter more fully into the reality of that strange birth in a stable.

Joseph, so runs the legend, hurries into the village to fetch a midwife. The woman comes and is astonished to find that her patient is a virgin. Back she rushes to tell her colleague, Salome, who mocks her. In retribution (exactly the kind of thing God never does) Salome finds that her arm has withered. It is only when she touches the child, sorrowing, that her flesh becomes healed again. The intention of the story is a good one, illustrating as it does that lack of faith actually damages us, makes us less whole, and that being restored to belief brings us back to full integrity again.

But God is not punitive in his actions, and this is something His Son would spell out again and again. Perhaps the artist was aware of this. His little midwife holds the baby with a firm hand, a diminutive angel waits to hand her a diaper and Joseph, like the ox and the ass at the top, peers into this strange world with uncomprehending respect. It is a tender little work, and Mary is delightfully relaxed. Maybe, like any young woman who has given birth to her firstborn, she is watching to see how the midwife deals with the child's bodily needs, to learn from her. It is an image of secluded happiness, and the controlled riot of flowers around the border serves to underline the peaceful stillness within.

THE NATIVITY
Anon., *The Office of the Blessed Virgin Mary*, Modena, 14th Century

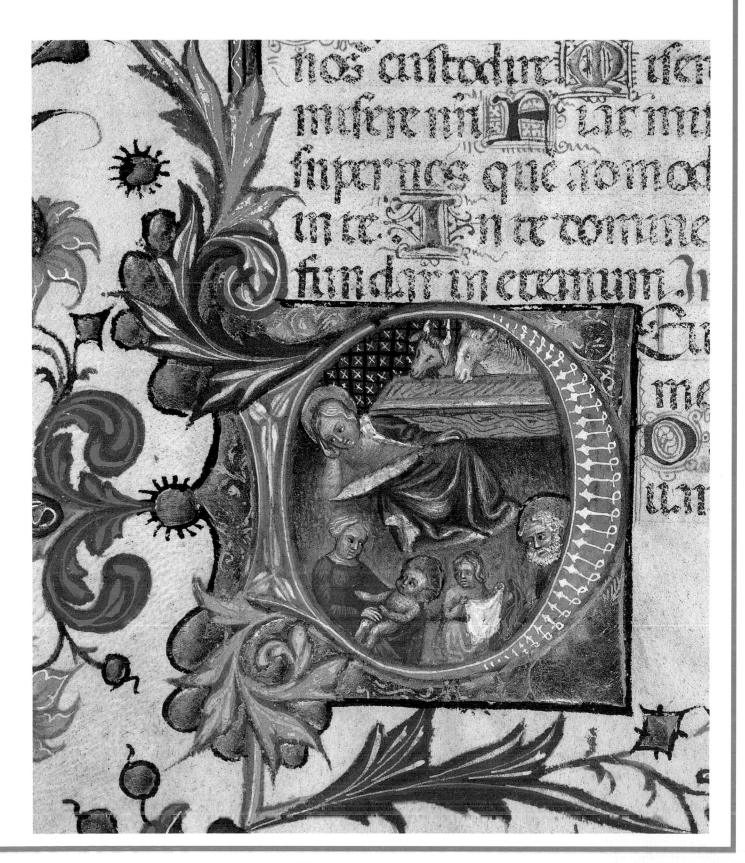

THE NATIVITY (IV)

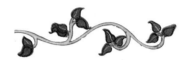

Here, with its hazy blues, reds, and indeterminate background colors, a great Byzantine artist elegantly sums up the essence of the Nativity narrative.

On the left runs the line of prophets, with David and his harp in the central position, flanked by Isaiah, who foretold that "a virgin shall conceive and be with child, and they will call his name Immanuel, God is with us," and by Micah, who said that the Messiah would be born in Bethlehem.

It mattered a great deal to the early church that Jesus was understood to have descended majestically from his Jewish background. It was Jesus who gave meaning to all that the prophets preached about God and his ways, hard as these sayings are to understand. (Saint Luke shows Jesus "opening the scriptures" to his companions after the Resurrection, and explaining to them all the passages that were about himself.)

The initial here is a giant B, and the top loop shows us Mary, her hands uplifted in holy astonishment as the angel, outside the confines of the letter, announces to her God's will. She is framed by the draped clothes of normal domesticity, an ordinary woman, called to an extraordinary service. We see what that service is in the lower part of the B. Mary and a pair of angels surround the sleeping Jesus while, at the very bottom, the midwife bathes the Savior . . . and learns to believe. Meanwhile, down the right-hand side, elongated and upside down, an insistent angel enlightens a dreaming Joseph, harassed as he is by the marginal beasts that surely symbolize his temptations. An animal and a child regard each other unperturbed in the lower left corner, showing that all the dramas and traumas ended in joy and peace.

This is a complex world, but it is presented, finally, as being integrated by a masterly hand.

THE NATIVITY
Anon., *Psalter*, Florence, early 13th Century

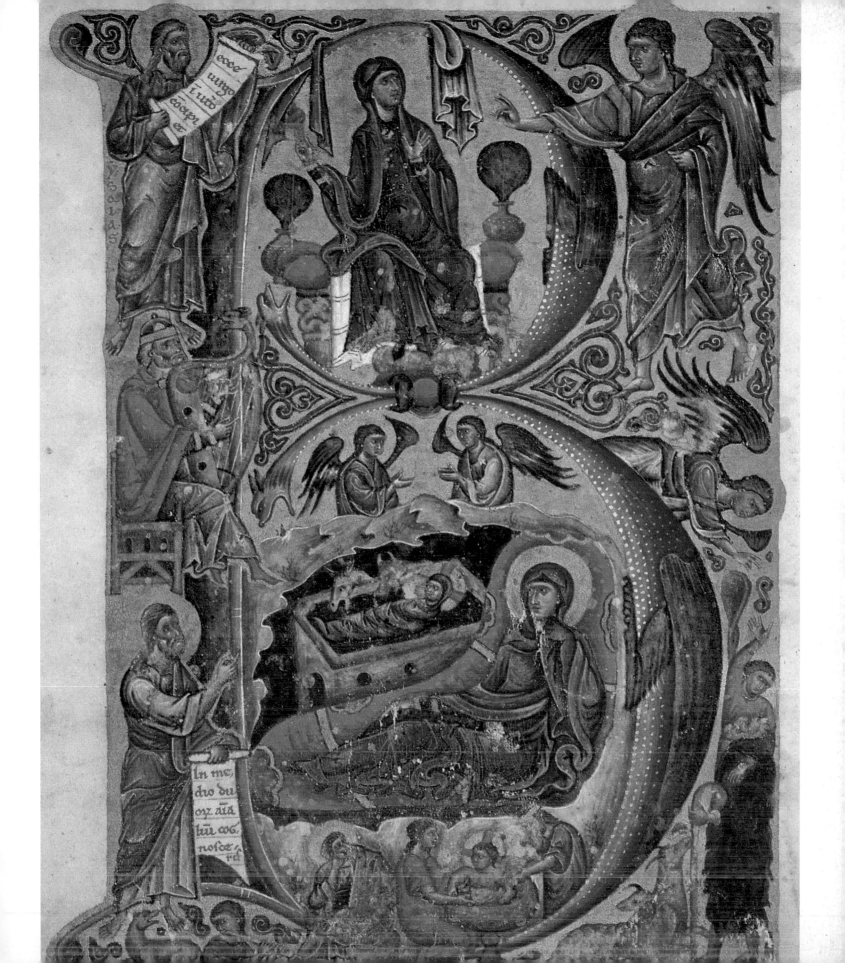

THE SHEPHERDS

"It really is the most extraordinary epiphany in literature, a lavishing of heavenly music and rapture upon a handful of illiterate Galileans to whom it came as a complete surprise."

The essence of the birth of Christ was that it was an event for everybody, not just for the privileged few, the Virgin and her saintly husband, who were its only witnesses.

Tradition has Christ born at midnight, but almost immediately after, "that very day," shepherds keeping a night watch over their sheep were suddenly enveloped in a terrifying splendor of angelic activity. The birth itself had been quiet and prayerful, a profoundly silent affair, it would seem. Now the "glory of the Lord" suddenly shines around these workaday peasants and they are accosted, not just by a single angel, telling them the news of this holy birth, but by a sky full of angels, "a great throng, praising God and singing: Glory to God in the highest and peace on earth to those who do His will." It really is the most extraordinary epiphany in literature, a lavishing of heavenly music and rapture upon a handful of illiterate Galileans to whom it came as a complete surprise.

The shepherds (who at the time had a rather dubious reputation, tending to be poachers on the side) accepted the message, made their way to Bethlehem, and had the grace to see the small newlyborn as the great God the angels announced. The poor, however slipshod their sense of mine and thine, were not found unworthy of their summons—a significant contrast to the wealthy and pious who, in later years, would reject the teachings of Christ and eventually condemn him to death.

The artist here does not portray matters so straightforwardly. Of the three shepherds, only one is alert to the angel. Several of his sheep have noticed the heavenly commotion as well—among them, we are pleased to see, a black one. But the other two shepherds, summoned to grace along with the first, equally enveloped in unearthly light, are intent only in their own hanky-panky. Granted, the bagpipe player does not encourage his persistent admirer, but he is nevertheless engrossed with her, her intrusive hands and her neat little person. If deafening choirs in the sky cannot catch their attention, there is small hope. The message, in other words, is always given, but not necessarily heeded. A desperate angel in the lower margin semaphores to them; he attracts the surprised gaze of the furthermost sheep, but the would-be lovers wrangle away in their blessedness.

THE ANNUNCIATION TO THE SHEPHERDS
Jacobus Coen attrib., *The Blessed Virgin Mary's Book of Hours*, Naples, pre-1550

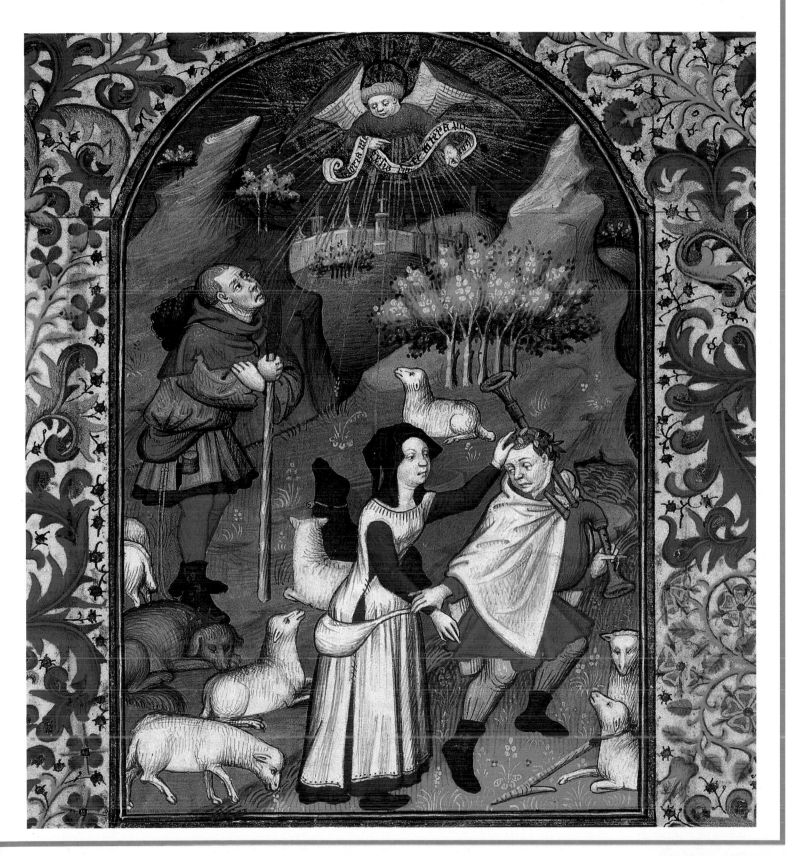

THE SHEPHERDS (II)

This artist sees the scene a little differently. The sheep are clearly not in on the action here, they are mere stage furniture, although there is an intelligent–looking dog. For intellect he may outrank the shepherds, both gaping gormlessly upward while an angel beckons wildly down at them and waves a lengthy scroll. "Glory to God in the highest," it reads, in case any of them are deaf and cannot hear the singing. The angel makes ardent gestures to the left, obviously the site of the stable, but the shepherds, in true rustic fashion, are not prepared to accept a stranger (particularly one not of this earth) too hastily. The artist has caught exactly that look of yokel bewilderment, the half-resentful response, that is typical of the illiterate and untraveled. The point being made here, though, is that in the eyes of the angels, we are all peasants, all out of our depth, all astonished and afraid to make fools of ourselves. Suppose it is all some sort of monstrous hoax? After all, what proof is there? How the fellows in the pub would laugh if we were taken in and actually obeyed the angel! The fear of Christianity being a myth that the sophisticated among us should be able to see through is still with us and always will be. The vacant look of the shepherd, neither believing nor disbelieving, unconsciously keeping his options open, will be mentally replicated by many who come after him. Can such "news of great joy" possibly be true? Is it not simply too good to be true?

As we know, the shepherds, after whatever debate and misgiving, did go to see what had happened—yet they saw nothing miraculous: They saw merely "Mary and Joseph and the baby lying in the manger": a virgin mother, a foster father and a divine child, but none of this singularity was visible to them. Faith, to be true faith, chooses to believe without proof. To these rough night birds goes the glory of having been the first to see Jesus and to know that he was more than mere man. The lying in the manger was a nice touch of holy economy, because one day the Child would give his body and blood as food to be eaten in Communion, though this further refinement of "good news" was never divulged to the shepherds.

THE ANNUNCIATION TO THE SHEPHERDS
Jacobus Coen attrib., *The Office of the Blessed Virgin Mary*, Turin, 15th Century

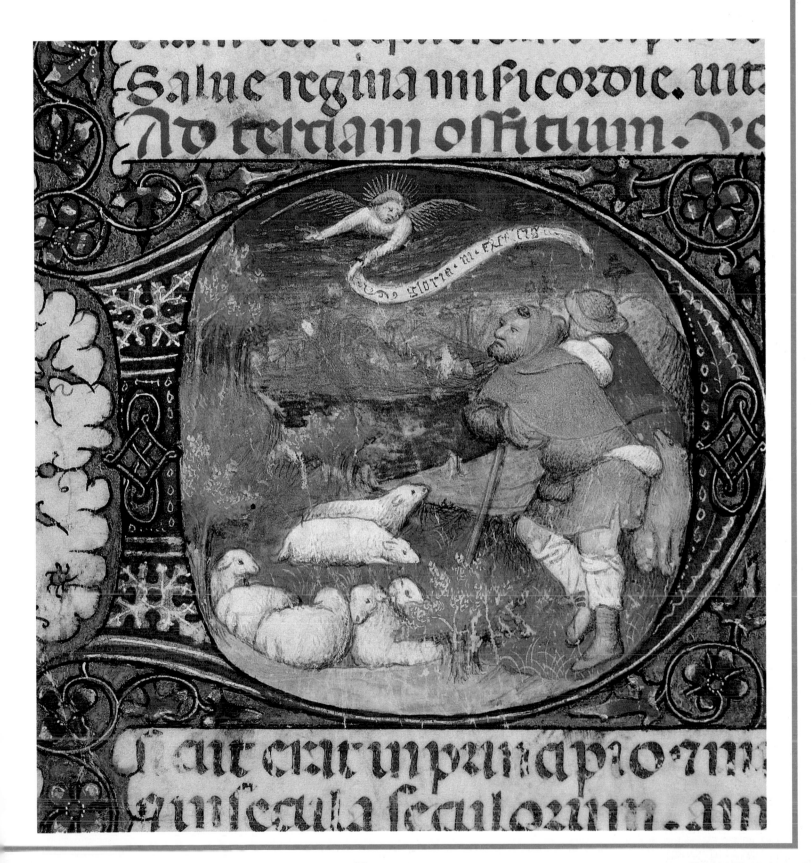

THE MAGI

If the shepherds are dramatically convincing, since they are the very people who would have been out that winter night in the fields, the presence of the Magi or kings seem fantastical. The arrival of these fairy-tale strangers from the East, these "wise men" or "Magi," journeying to greet Jesus because of a star they had observed in their homeland, is an unprecedented event.

For Saint Matthew, the only evangelist who writes about these exotic visitors, they are the palpable embodiment of the mysterious prophecy of Isaiah, centuries before, that "kings will come…to your light…camels in throngs …dromedaries of Midian and Epaah…bringing gold and incense…." Of course these kings came, reasoned Saint Matthew, though he called them only "wise men" and gave us little detail beyond the nature of their gifts: gold, of course, incense, and precious myrrh. Christian imagination has played happily with these ideas, giving the kings names (Balthasar, Melchior, and Caspar) and arranging them in meaningful patterns. One is old, one middle-aged, one youthful, and one is from the East, one from the distant West, and one, the most romantic of all, is a dark man from Africa.

Once again, as with the shepherds, the real point of the story is that the wise men saw nothing exceptional to force their faith. They saw Mary and the child, poorly housed in their crude, open stable, with a suspicious Joseph glowering at them from beneath his cap; well–dressed foreigners, armed with expensive presents, seem to home–keeping Joseph to need careful watching. Mary is simply astonished, and even the little Jesus looks taken aback, as if this human life is hard to get to grips with. The kings stand silent in adoration— their noble gifts their only credentials. Each seems bemused by how much greater the event is than they could have expected.

Their furs and satins, their golden crowns and exotic turbans, seem mere tinsel in the presence of this naked child and his mouse of a mother. Low on his knees, the senior king acts out the overthrow of human certainties and the arrival of a new order.

THE ADORATION OF THE MAGI
Anon., *The Office of the Blessed Virgin Mary's Book of Hours,* Turin, late 15th Century

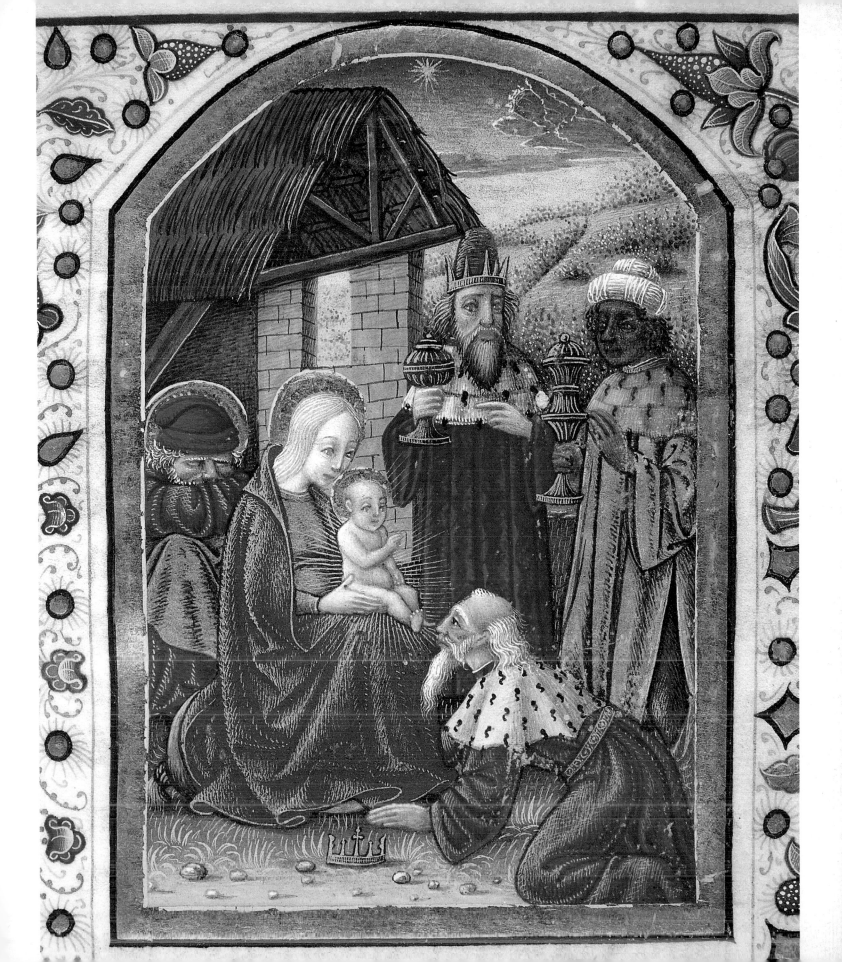

THE MAGI (II)

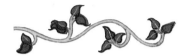

Although historical reports of Herod's reign make no mention of them, the Magi play an important role in the story of the early years, as Saint Matthew sees them. A line from the prophet Hosea, that God called to his son "out of Egypt," invites the question of how Jesus, who was later to say that his immediate mission was only to the lost sheep of Israel, could ever have traveled there. Matthew solves this, and other prophecies too (that there would be "mourning and loud lamentation" for lost children), by explaining the consequences of this kingly visit.

As was natural, the kings had gone first to Herod, expecting to find there the newborn "King of the Jews." The wily Herod sent them away, after which the star reappeared to lead them to Bethlehem, but he had made them promise to return and tell him the whereabouts of the child so that he, too, might go and worship. An angel warned the kings to go home by another route, since Herod's plans were murderous. Here, as they innocently make their way back to Jerusalem, the angel halts them and turns the whole cavalcade round.

Unfortunately, this particular artist portrays only white–skinned kings, though there is a dandy of a black page in their entourage, leading a supercilious and intelligent dromedary, who seems to have suspected a plot from the start. Before their horses lies a strangely star-shaped object, as if to tell us that the star has done its work and their task is now to escape with their message of faith. However we interpret it, this long journey across uncharted deserts, indicated by the rocky paths, represents an enormous investment in the search for truth. This is a story of incredible perseverance, earnestness, and the rewards that follow.

The good news came easily to the shepherds: it caused many difficulties for these distant scholars, who made great sacrifices of time and energy, all to track down a possibility. Remote in their eastern lands, they would never have heard of Christ, but they studied, they worried, and they pondered on the meaning of the star. They took active steps to solve the mystery, and they found what they sought.

THE ADORATION OF THE MAGI
Cristoforo de Predis, *Concerning the Life of Saint Joachim . . .*, Turin, 1476

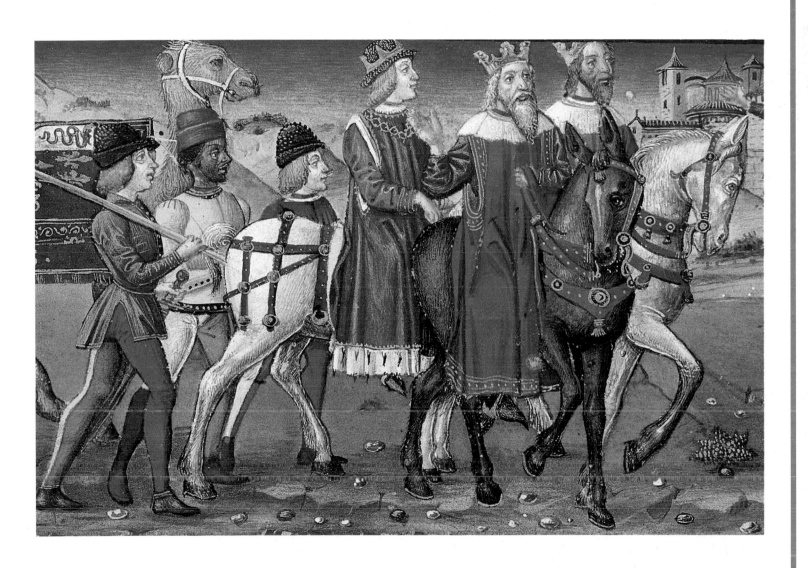

JESUS AMONG US

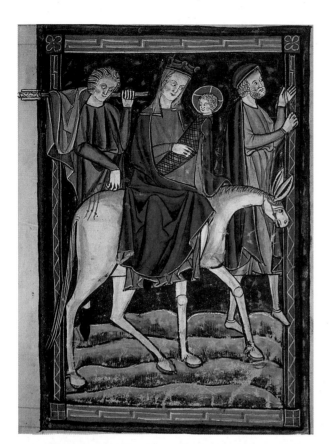

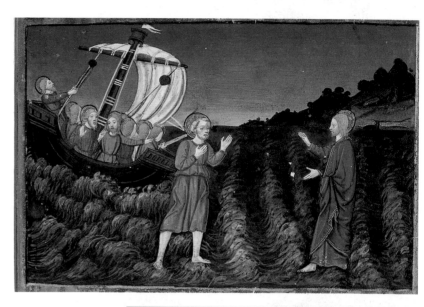

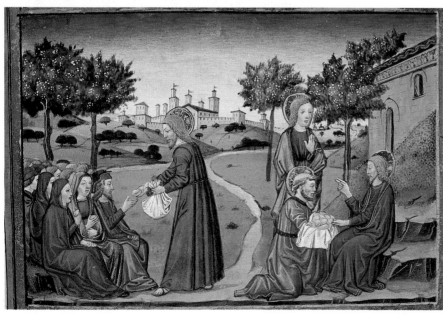

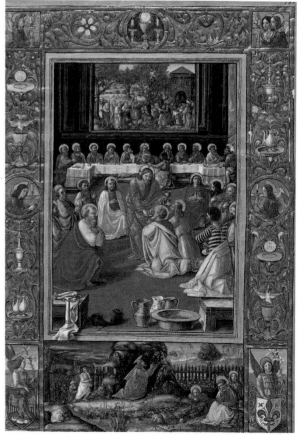

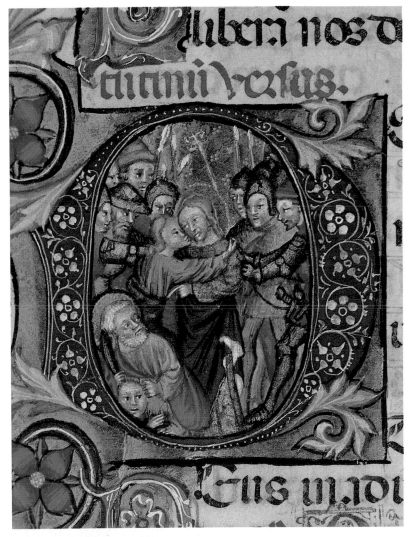

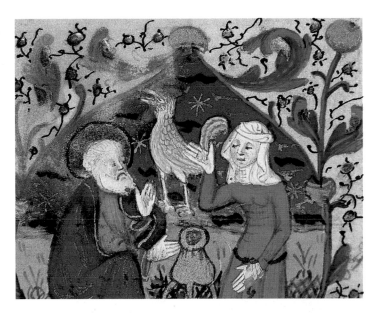

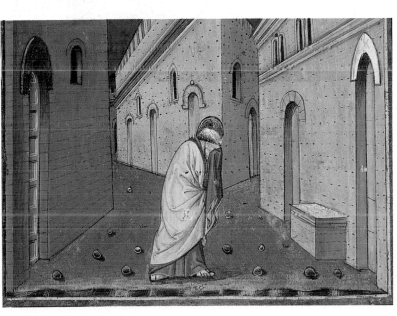

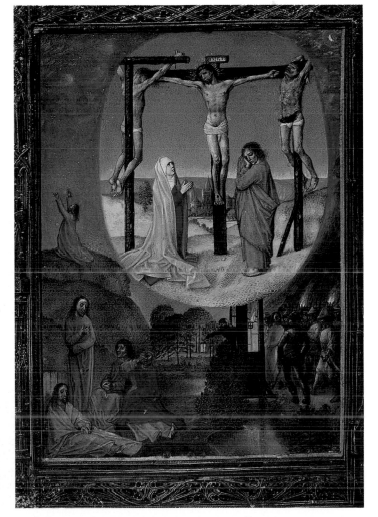

THE FLIGHT INTO EGYPT

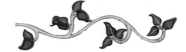

The Magi escaped, and took safely with them the secret of the child's whereabouts, but Herod was a psychopath whose fears loomed the larger for their very lack of clarity. His solution to the problem of not knowing which child to kill was simple— kill them all, every boy-child under two.

Joseph, prudent and watchful, had already heard the rumors and whisked his family away to Egypt overnight. Mary agrees to go into exile, but in the confidence that, one day, God will call them home again.

The artist surrounds the fleeing family with scenes of slaughter: a child as young as Jesus is snatched from his mother's arms just a stone's throw from the path on which they hasten away, while at the bottom of the page we see the drama played out in all its cruelty. Herod, regal and suspicious, sends a soldier with sword at the ready, commanding him to hunt down the terrified mother whom we see trying to run off the page and out of the story. Above, in the margins, a bird presides with indifference over these examples of human

THE MASSACRE OF THE HOLY INNOCENTS
The Massacre of the Holy Innocents is celebrated by the church every year, three days after Christmas. These innocent babies, the church holds, gave their lives for Christ by dying so that he might live.

torture, while at the upper right, a ferocious lion has a long-nosed human face. Man becomes brute. In the center, though, a grieving Mary carries her small package of a child to safety.

In the far background the artist even manages to illustrate one of the Flight into Egypt legends. The Holy Family is said to have passed a farmer sowing corn, and when Herod's men asked him if he had seen any escapees, he answered truthfully that nobody had gone by since he sowed his crop. But miraculously, the crop had sprung up and was ready for reaping, which completely threw the villains off the scent, while preventing the farmer from telling a lie.

THE FLIGHT INTO EGYPT
Anon., *The Blessed Virgin Mary's Book of Hours,*
Turin, 15th Century

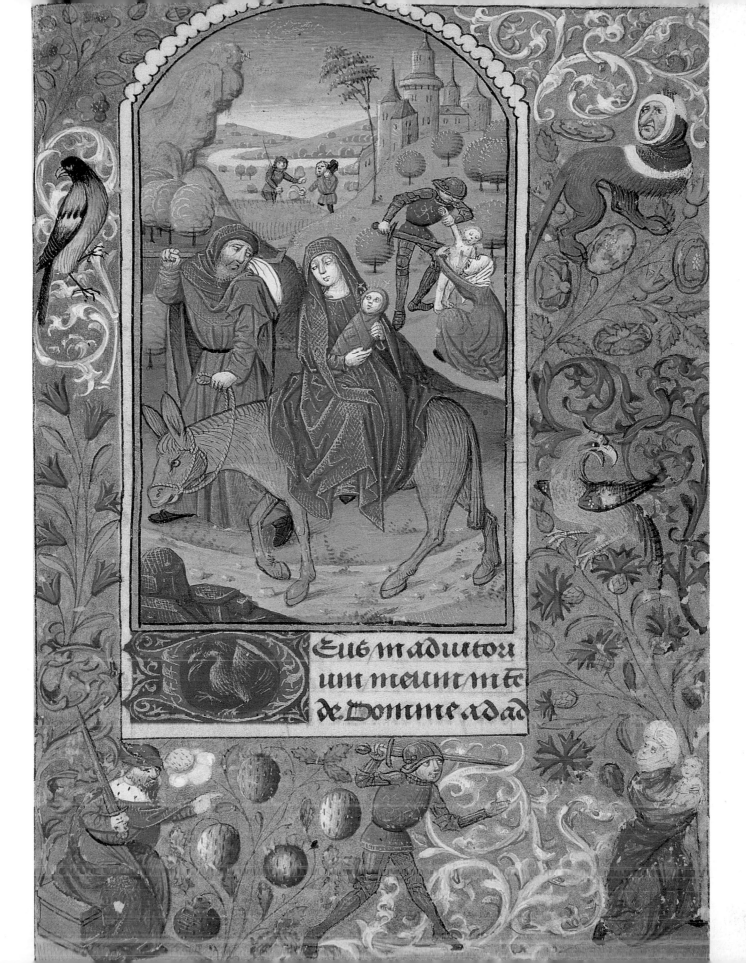

Eus madiutori
um mentint
de nomme adad

THE FLIGHT INTO EGYPT (II)

Jesus, who is to end his life by dying for others, begins it by having others die for him. His safety is bought at the cost of a heap of mutilated babies, and his mother's happiness has been preserved by the terrible misery experienced by other mothers.

The family is going into exile, and in this is no different from families of homeless refugees all over the world, in scenes so wretchedly familiar to us in our unhappy century. This may be the second millennium, but the fact is that Herods and their soldiers still abound, and so do dead children.

We cannot imagine this artist reducing his great theme to the level of legend, however charming. He invites us to contemplate, with Mary and her husband, the compromises of living. They cannot save the massacred children: to turn back would merely add yet another small corpse to Herod's pile. It is their duty to run away, however unheroic, and at whatever terrible cost to others.

The Holy Family has escaped from the immediate threat of slaughter. The artist is painfully aware of the implicit irony in this.

All the characters here seem to be reflecting on this, from a tragic Joseph, a pensive Mary, and an impassive Jesus, to the donkey, showing us only a mournfully gleaming eye. The sinister feel of the picture suggests that the world into which Mary has brought her son is not a safe one. It offers no easy choices, and there is no way through it that will not inflict pain, on oneself or on others.

The artist is deeply conscious that there is no simple way of resolving life's dreadful dilemmas; each dilemma has to be taken in prayer to God, where each will find its answer. Joseph was instructed "in a dream" to take the child and his mother and flee to Egypt, but, dream or vision, inward conviction or rational deduction, prayer will never leave us without a way forward. What is never promised is that the way will be simple or consoling. Mary may have mourned for those other mothers all her life.

THE FLIGHT INTO EGYPT
Anon., *Psalter*, Venice, 1270–80

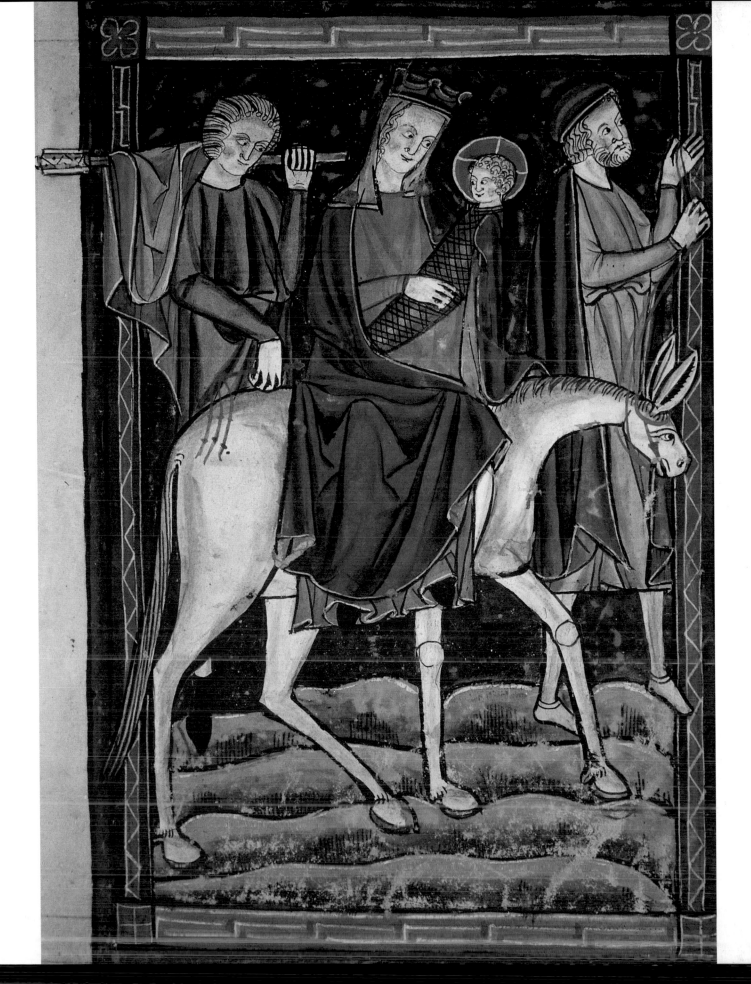

THE FEEDING OF THE FIVE THOUSAND

W hat came next, after the birth, after the great event? Two of the evangelists, Saints Mark and John, ignore the birth stories and begin their accounts with an adult Jesus, already intent on preaching the gospel: "For this was I born and for this I came into the world, that I might bear witness to the truth." "Truth" is at the centre of Christ's being, the truth that "sets us free," since it grounds us in our own integrity and inspires us with the conviction of the Father's love. The books of illuminated prayer rarely dwell on anything outside the crucial events of Christ's life, highlighting a story here and there, on the way from crib to cross—hence the rarity of miracle pictures. But the Feeding of the Five

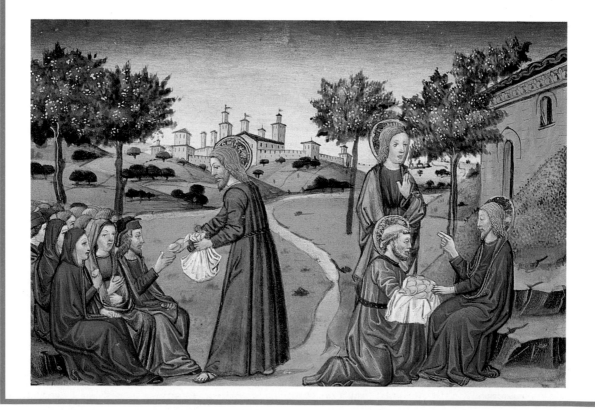

"Whole baskets of unwanted bread are left over, and the crowd comes gratefully to thank Jesus for their hearty meal."

Thousand had direct relevance to the Last Supper and the gift of the Eucharist, and here is a delightful before and after image.

The first picture shows the pathetic packet of loaves (the fish are written out, to make the Eucharistic reference more obvious), offered to Jesus in despair. "This is all there is," says Saint Andrew, "but what is that among so many?" Scene one, then: Jesus solemnly blesses the loaves. Scene two: an apostle grits his teeth at the fool he is making of himself and starts along the line of hungry people, distributing food. In another miniature (not shown), we have the result: whole baskets of unwanted

bread are left over, and the crowd comes gratefully to thank Jesus for its hearty meal. The artist sees this as a communion meal—witness the reverence with which each receives the bread and the attitude of prayerful awe with which they offer their thanks to Jesus. The apostles have acted out the roles of priests at a Eucharist, but it is Jesus who said the "words of consecration": he is the true priest, the only priest, who empowers his disciples to act in His name. Saint John does not even describe the Last Supper, with its breaking and blessing of the bread—the "body" of Christ. He feels the whole story to be conveyed in this miracle.

left and below:
THE FEEDING OF THE FIVE THOUSAND
Cristoforo de Predis, *Concerning the Life of Saint Joachim . . . ,* Turin, 1476

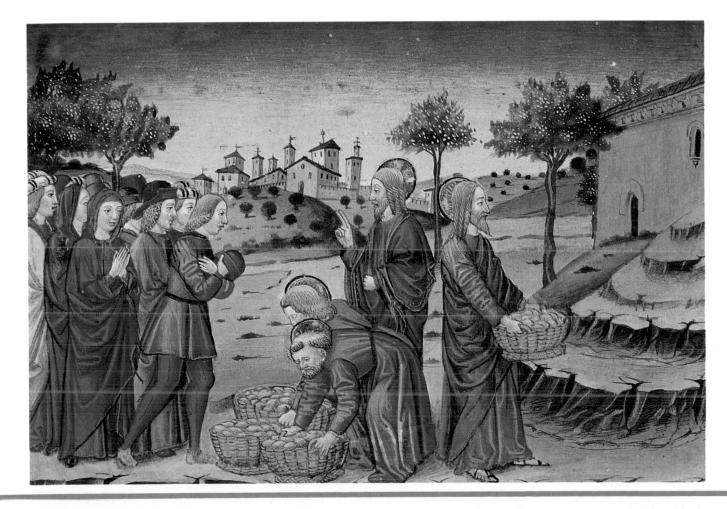

PETER WALKING ON THE WATER

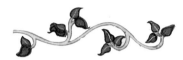

"Salvation —the state of being changed from within into the person we were meant to be—is not within our own power."

Prayer that concentrates on the specific runs the risk of being disappointed: God answers the total need of the heart, which we may never have identified, even to ourselves. There will always be an answer, even a miraculous one, but the form it takes may be disconcerting.

The first image shows the terrified apostles, caught in a storm without Jesus. They have one specific plea—they want to be saved. Peter, as their leader, articulates this. While the others are in a state of noisy panic, Peter observes what seems to be the miraculous answer to his prayer: he sees Jesus walking toward them on the water, telling them not to be afraid. Then he has misgivings: can this really be Jesus? Brashly and rashly, he safeguards his belief behind a

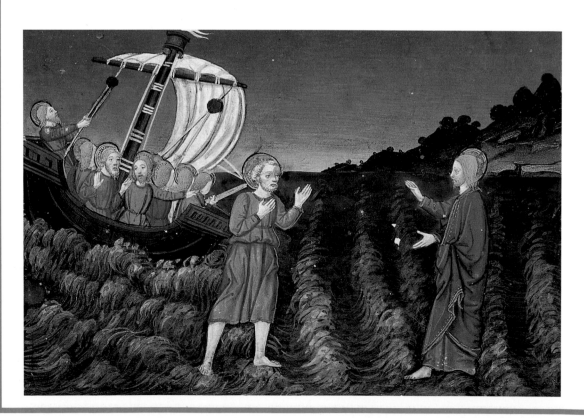

challenge: "Lord, if it be thou, bid me to come to thee upon the water." Jesus answers him: "Come," and Peter, eyes set on his Lord, steps out onto the waves. Fatally, Peter takes his eyes off Jesus and turns them on himself. The obvious impossibility of walking on water strikes him with such force that he immediately begins to sink and, as the second image shows, Jesus must fish him out with a quiet reprimand.

The point is not that Jesus can work miracles and that the sea is his to command. It is rather that we are always safe and only safe if we fix our attention on God and not on our own deficiencies. Salvation—the state of being changed from within into the person we were meant to be—is not within our own power. Self-conscious breast-beating about our failings and inadequacies will get us nowhere. After all, no one knows better than God how pitiful is our spiritual strength. But we are not meant to live in our own strength, but in that of Another. When Saint Paul writes to the church at Philippi that "it is God who is at work within you, giving you the will and the power to achieve His purpose," he is delivering the same message as that portrayed in this story. Faith demands that we forget about ourselves, which is something we, like Peter, find very difficult.

left and below:
THE STILLING OF THE STORM
Cristoforo de Predis, *Concerning the Life of Saint Joachim...,* Turin, 1476

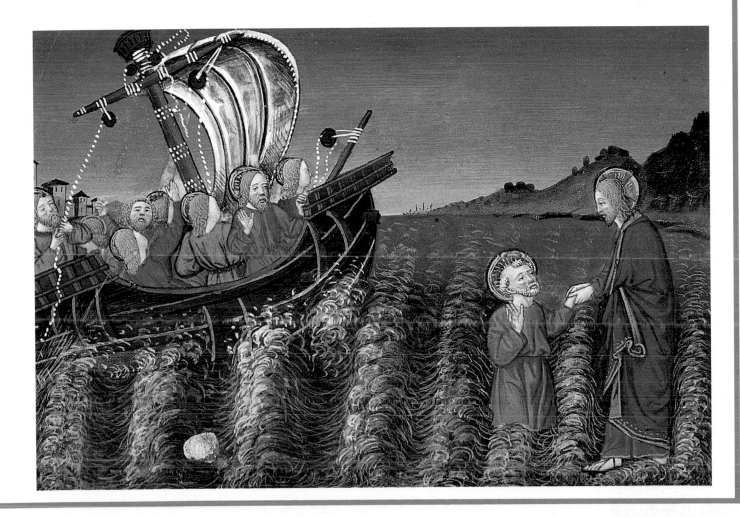

THE LAST SUPPER

"These brilliant yellows, blues, reds, and the dazzling white all speak of triumph, not defeat."

This is an ambitious picture, perhaps a little overambitious, since the artist has tried to include four different events of Passiontide. Inset into the back wall is a brightly colored representation of Palm Sunday, with Jesus riding on an ass and being greeted with wild enthusiasm by the Jerusalem crowd that would disown him a few days later. In the center are shown two stages in the Last Supper itself. We see Jesus still at table, blessing the bread, with John leaning on his shoulder and Judas hostile on the opposite side of the table. In the foreground of the major image we have Jesus feeding his friends on this sacred and mysterious food. Below, we see the Lord agonizing in the garden of Gethsemane later that night, alone in his struggle to accept the terrible will of his loving Father, while Judas creeps onstage with the band of soldiers who will arrest him.

All around the margin of the picture are hosts and chalices, interspersed with grieving angels who bear lilies and lighted candles. The symbolism is dense, and this may be apt in its heaviness. These Holy Thursday events are too weighty to be analyzed easily. The only genuine

THE COMMUNION

Whether we call it the Mass or the Eucharist, a Communion Service or a Meal of Reconciliation, the Last Supper is at the heart of the Christian faith. On the night before he entered into his Passion, Jesus invited his disciples to feed on bread and wine that he had blessed. This was His Body and His Blood. "Do this," he said, "in memory of me," and so the church has, ever since.

response is to pray, to unite with the suffering Jesus and to affirm our faith in his life and death. This is what the birth, in all its simplicity and joy, leads up to. Death is, after all, implicit in birth, and as far as the pain of death or the body's dispossession goes, Jesus did indeed die. The gift of his body and separated blood, given as food and drink, was made while he was still alive. It was an offering, a gift of himself, not an involuntary wrenching away from life, as death usually seems for us.

The theme may be tragic, but this picture communicates an inner hopefulness through colour. The brilliant yellows, blues, reds, and the dazzling white all speak of triumph, not defeat.

THE LAST SUPPER
Monte di Giovanni di Miniato di Gherardo,
Missal, **Florence, 1494–1502**

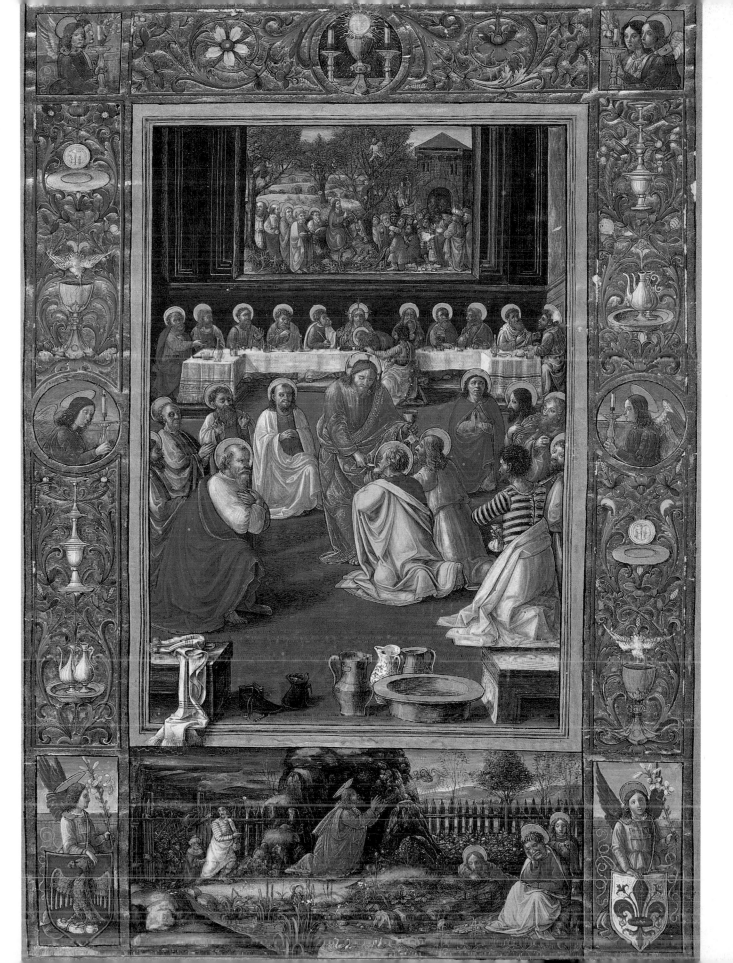

JUDAS' BETRAYAL

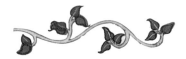

> *"We are being asked here to examine not the problem of Judas and his sin but the problem of our own."*

In this picture, Jesus, hands at rest amidst a swarm of armored soldiers, is flanked by two men. Both are among his closest friends and followers. On the right we see Peter, vehement in defense and raising a sword to attack the high priest's servant, Malchus, who stands in front of him. It is a futile gesture, based not in faith but in fear. If Peter had truly believed that Jesus was the Son of God, then he would have known that violence in the "service" of religion is inherently pointless. Jesus taught his followers to love, and aggression has no place here.

Even sadder is the figure on the left, seen moving away from the group into the loneliness of remorse. Judas, for whatever reason, has betrayed his Master. At the Last Supper, Jesus made it clear that he knew of this intention. He made no attempts to change Judas's mind: this was to be an act of personal responsibility, as are all our acts. But as the traitor arrives with his soldiers, Jesus addresses him still—and, it would seem, always—as: Friend. Judas may have turned away from Jesus, but Jesus has not turned away from Judas. Even here, his eyes seem to follow Judas's departure, sadly and silently. The man dressed in red holding the lantern brutally spotlights this stiff-necked departure, away from the circle milling round Christ and out into his own secret darkness.

Artists have traditionally been hard on Judas the traitor, often portraying him as so obvious a villain as to raise doubts about his initial eligibility for apostleship. Here the artist is more logical—and more chilling.

The horror of Judas is not that he was unlike the other disciples but that he was just like them. He enjoyed all their advantages, above all the personal closeness to Jesus. Yet he could choose to deny him.

We are being asked here to examine not the problem of Judas and his sin but the problem of our own: why do we betray, and walk away?

JUDAS'S BETRAYAL OF JESUS
Anon., *The Office of the Blessed Virgin Mary*, Modena, 14th Century

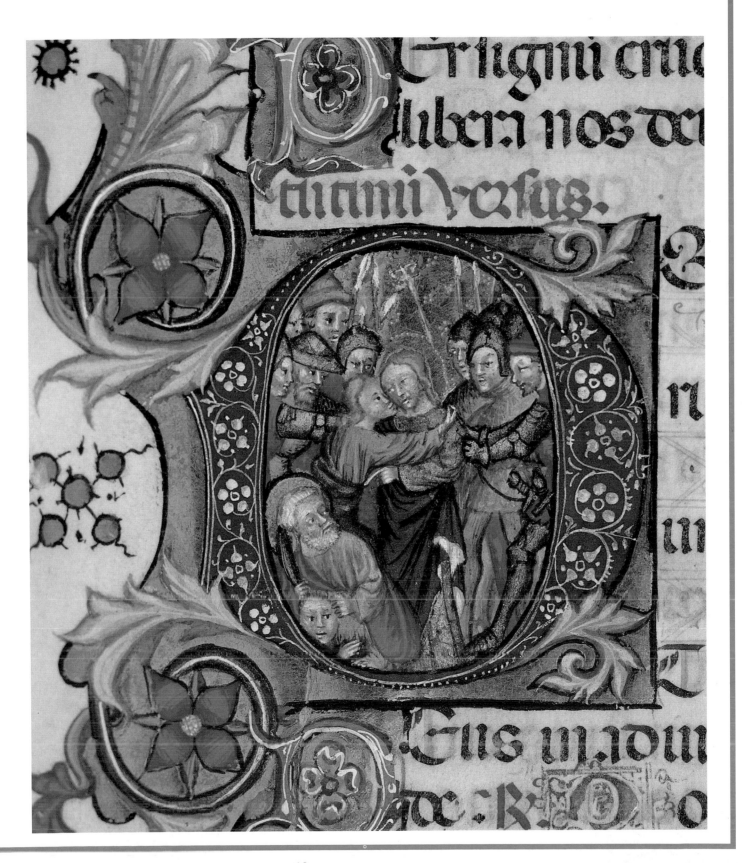

PETER'S DENIAL

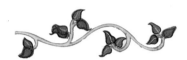

> *"Here he touches bottom, and yet we notice that the artist still—and rightly—shows him with a halo, tattered but nevertheless real."*

When Jesus is betrayed to death, Judas is the villain and Peter, in his own eyes at least, is the hero. His impulsive and ill-judged swipe with a sword, seen in the last picture, is the only "defense" that Jesus receives. But it is short-lived.

As we already know from the gospels, Peter is inconsistent in his attitude—he is in fighting mode one minute, and the next he is for flight, joining the other apostles in their swift retreat. But, again typically, he cannot stay away from his Lord Jesus. His devotion, however flawed, is genuine and he must have remembered often how he had boasted to Jesus that "even if all betray you, I will never betray you." Jesus told him (we can imagine he spoke with a wry smile) that "before the cock crows twice, you will deny me three times."

This poignant little picture shows us the crowing cock in his triumph and Peter, no longer crowing, in his disgrace. He did indeed deny his master, three times insisting to the servant girl in the courtyard of the High Priest's house that he knew nothing of Jesus. He had only come to that courtyard so as to be near the Lord, who was on trial for his life

indoors, and he joined the servants clustered around the fire, keeping warm through a long and chilly night. His Galilean accent gave him away, and one of the men had actually seen him with Jesus. Peter, terrified, denied the servant girl's accusations again and again.

The artist depicts the servant as essentially unmalicious, merely a skeptical young woman who knows a liar when she sees one. Peter counters her hand language with furious vigor, "cursing and swearing."

The rather wobbly stove around which both stand has a symbolic significance as well. Peter will soon hear that accusatory crowing, will suddenly realize what he has done and will be overwhelmed by the red-hot anguish of bitter sorrow. Yet it is this moment of shame, at the faint threat of a slender young woman, both charming and harmless, that finally and forever alerts Peter to the truth of his own weakness. Here he touches bottom, and yet we notice that the artist still—and rightly—shows him with a halo, tattered but nevertheless real.

THE PREDICTION OF PETER'S DENIAL
Anon., *The Office of the Blessed Virgin Mary,*
Florence, 1420–30

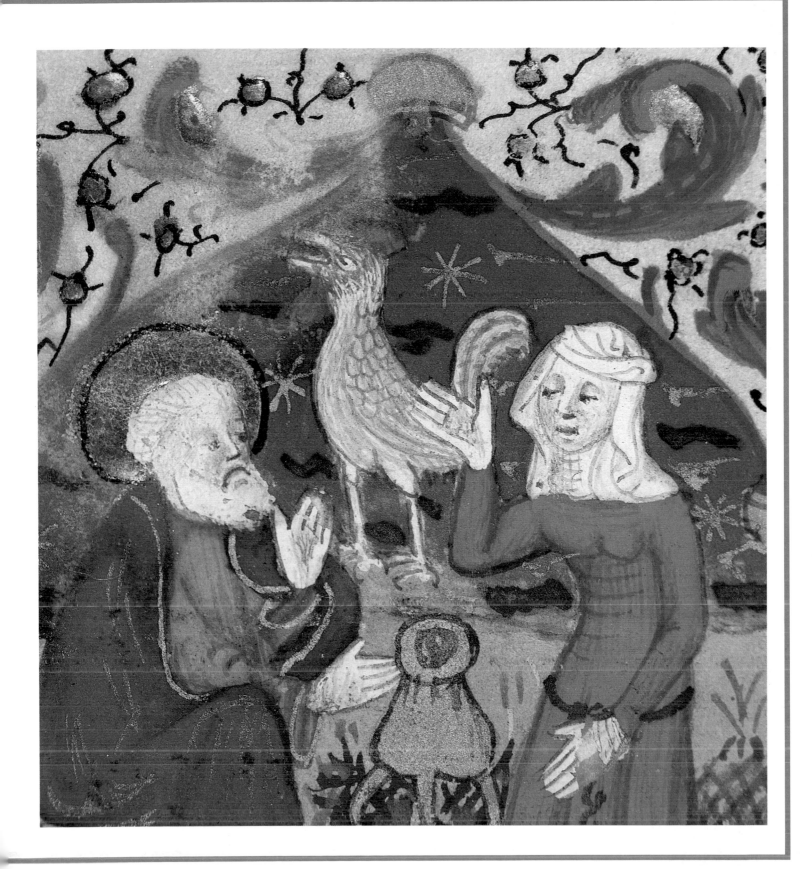

PETER'S REPENTANCE

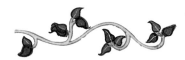

The famous scene in the garden courtyard, where Peter three times vehemently denied that he had any knowledge of Jesus, ended when the guards brought their prisoner out. Saint Luke tells us that "the Lord turned and looked at Peter, and he remembered." The gospel continues sadly: "and he went out and wept bitterly."

This magical little picture presents an unforgettable image of grief. It is that most painful kind of grief, lamenting of our own folly. Tradition has it that years of weeping scored deep furrows down Peter's cheeks, but here we see him with his shamed face covered, stumbling blindly forward from one closed door to the next. There are ways out behind him, but Peter is too lost in misery to look for them. He bruises his feet on the pebbles as he lurches away from his nightmare of infidelity. This claustrophobic despair, this helpless anguish, this incapacitating sense of shame: these are the result of a sudden overturn of our own self-image.

Peter had honestly seen himself as one who loved and followed Jesus, priding himself, moreover, on how true his loyalty was in comparison with that of others. "Even if all should betray you, I will never betray you"—it was a boast, but he had meant it. Now he sees, piercingly, that he is fraudulent.

We suspect that it is not only fear for Jesus that racks Peter, though that element would surely have been present in his tears. He now fears for himself, less for his life than for his integrity; he has been unmasked to himself, he has lost his self-worth.

The crucial question is: What next? Will he hide his face forever, destroyed by self-pity, that most deadly of vices? Will he lose all heart, perhaps even kill himself, as Judas did (another man wracked by grief)? But while Judas felt only remorse, which consumed itself in pointless repining, Peter feels contrition, a healing sorrow that will lead to repentance and a change of heart. Now that he knows his true weakness, he will cling to Jesus as never before. He will cling in desperate need and not in false strength, and will in the end become truly Peter, the "rock," on which the church, likewise dependent on Christ, will be built.

PETER'S REPENTANCE
Cristoforo de Predis, *Concerning the Life of Saint Joachim . . .* , Turin, 1476

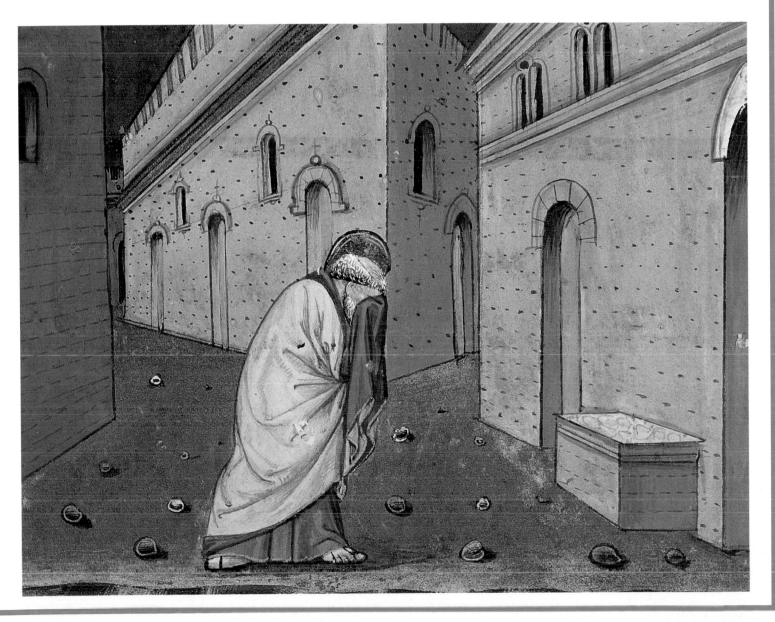

THE PASSION

Like a great elongated moon, the night sky is filled with the Crucifixion. There hangs Jesus, flanked by the two thieves, one of whom will die rejecting him and the other, equally criminal, who will die with those wonderful words from Jesus in his ears: "This day thou shalt be with me in Paradise."

At any moment, even literally our last, we can become different. Saint John stands beneath the cross, unable to watch his Lord suffer, and Mary kneels, in a position very similar to that in which we have seen her so often in the Nativity scenes. She knelt in prayer and joy bedside her naked son when he was born, and now kneels as, naked once again, he dies. The pure, bright light brings the tragedy into sharp focus; it is high noon, and the very courtyard seems overexposed and colorless in the merciless heat. The one color present is the red of John's robe.

In stark contrast, the world shown beneath this hanging oval is soft with the darkness of night. Light glimmers romantically on water and from torches, but it is a false romance. This is the light of betrayal, as Judas leads the soldiers to capture Jesus in the solitude of heart that must not have been new to him. Saint John reports Jesus saying sadly at the Last Supper that he has been with them "so long a time, and you still do not know me." Here on the mountain, Jesus lifts up his arms in agonized petition to the Father, who alone does truly know him. He pleads to be spared "this cup," and the inset picture of death is probably the vision that fills his mind as he prays.

Jesus's evident struggle to accept pain and death must encourage us all. He did not choose torture: he was a normal, vulnerable man, just like ourselves. But once it was clear that it was to be, he accepted it totally and went forward to his terrible death with peaceful dignity.

In the lower left corner of the picture he wakens his sleeping disciples to warn them of what is to come, and to tell them of their need for prayer. Then the ominous torches on the right break in upon the stillness and Jesus begins the lonely path to his death.

THE CRUCIFIXION
Simon Marmion, Gheraert Heronbout, Alexander Bening attrib., *The Blessed Virgin Mary's Book of Hours,* Naples, 1483–98

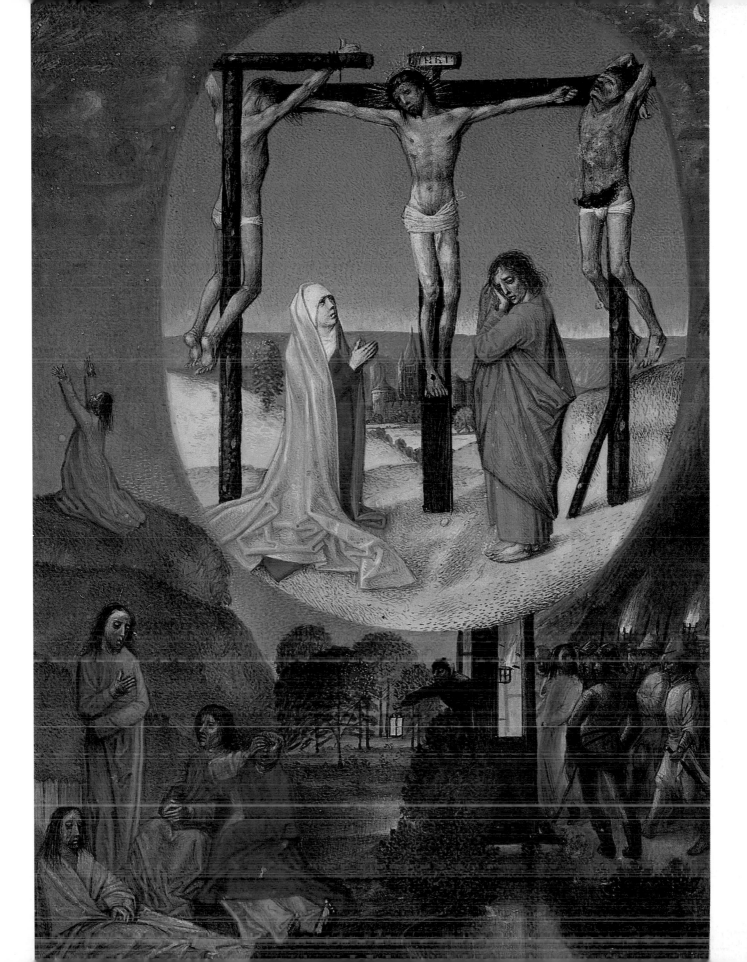

DEATH AND RESURRECTION

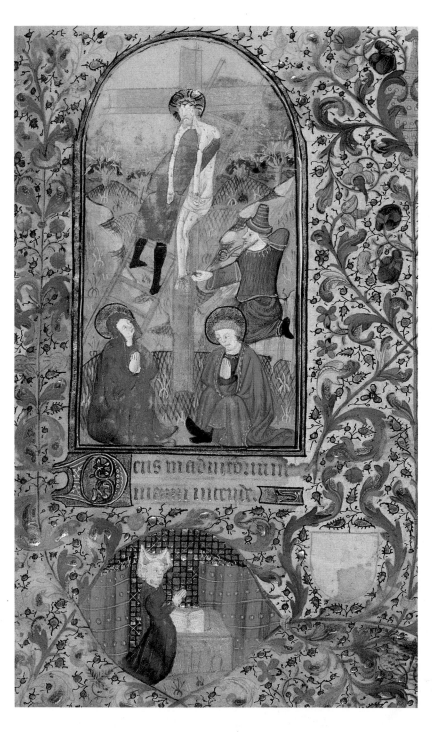

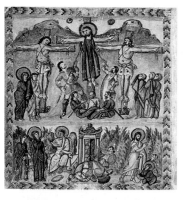

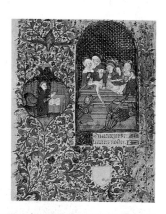

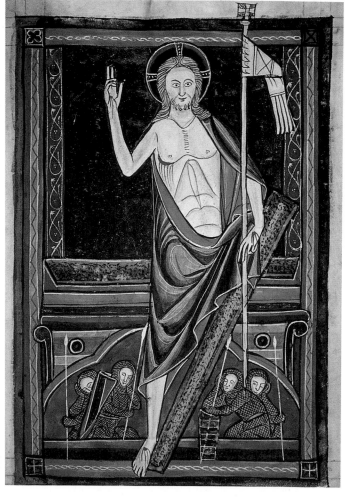

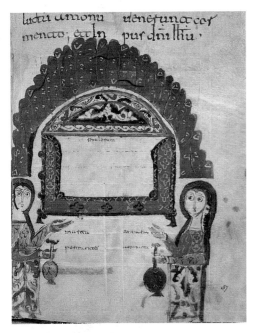

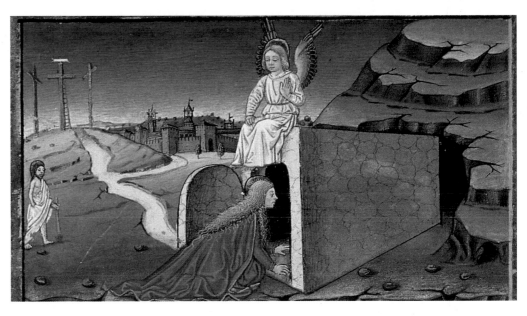

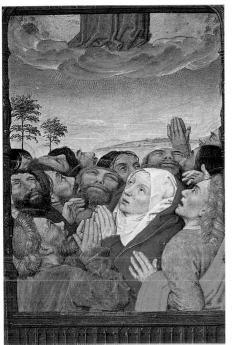

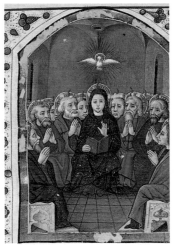

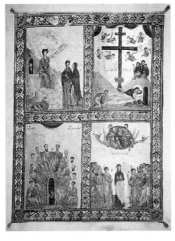

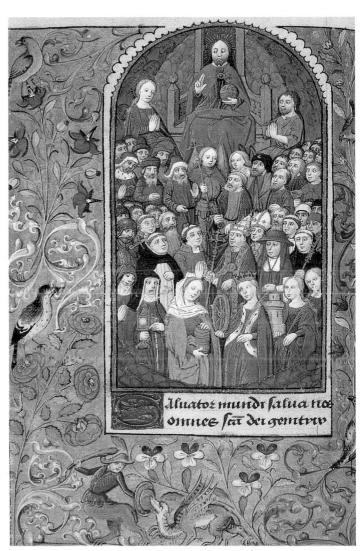

THE DEPOSITION

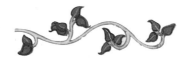

> *"Jesus has descended into the abyss, but only to rise up from it, with death forever conquered."*

For centuries, Christian art could not bring itself to show Christ dead. He was depicted as still in command, ruling from the cross, commanding and unhurt.

Even when death was accepted emotionally (since theology left no loophole here), it was somehow a beautiful death, with a relaxed Jesus seeming to sleep with his dignity intact. Real death is not like that: it is pathetic and utterly without dignity. The person who controlled that body has left it, and only the shell remains.

This artist has dared to look straight at death. He is not a master of form, and this is more a diagram of death than a true representation, but it is nevertheless frighteningly convincing. Jesus sags onto the arms that lift him down from the cross.

We know the names of the two eminent Jews who came to bury Jesus: Joseph of Arimathea and Nicodemus. One is pulling out the nails from the Lord's feet—he is a compact bundle of unsentimental compassion. The other is smothered by the descending weight that collapses limply down upon him. Jesus is bloodless, a long thin figure, utterly dead.

The artist's lack of skill may be an advantage here in that we cannot determine whether the man on the ladder (Joseph or Nicodemus?) is clutching Jesus or embracing him. Perhaps the passionate hold is both—an intense grasp that speaks of love as well as support. The ladder has slipped sideways, underlying the instability of the action. John, sitting in prayer, is rapt in his sorrow, but Mary looks sadly up. At some level, even if not fully conscious, could she be aware that her son will not remain dead, that this scene is unstable in a deeper sense?

Jesus has descended into the abyss, but only to rise up from it with death forever conquered. Already the trees in the background are starting to flower, and the margins of the miniature almost buckle under the burgeoning pressure of the surrounding page. Here life is on hold, dreadfully so, but has not gone away eternally.

THE DEPOSITION
Anon., *The Office of the Blessed Virgin Mary*, Florence, 1420–30

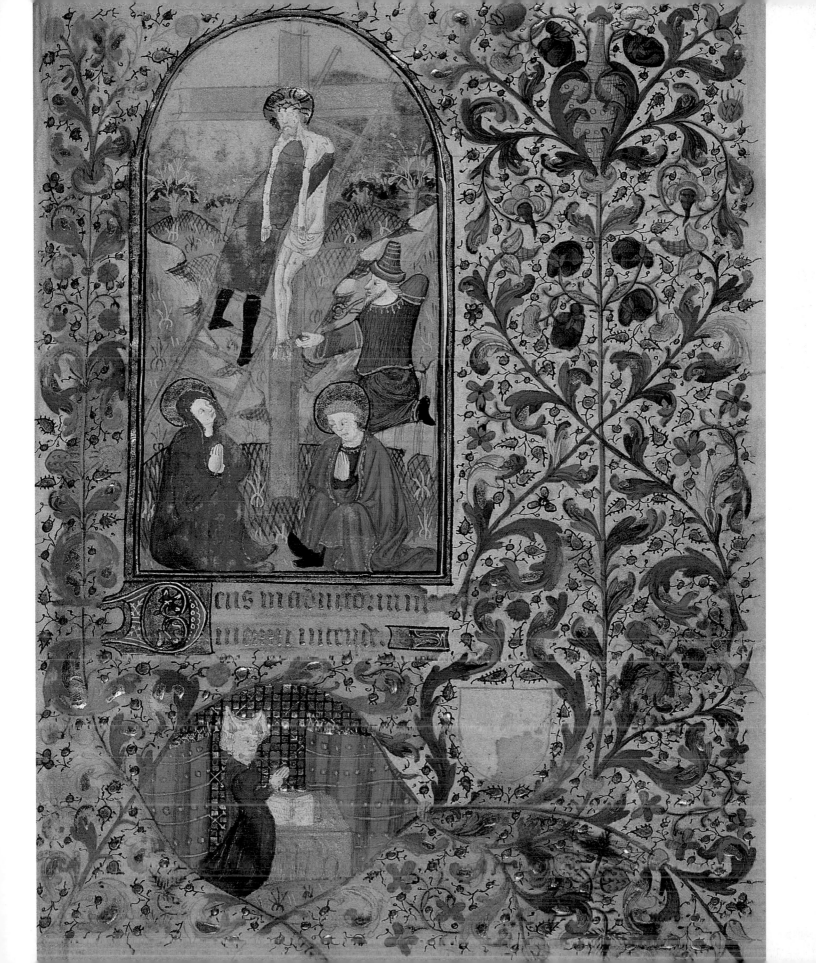

JESUS IS LAID IN THE TOMB

"It may be merely artistic ineptitude, but the unrealistic jutting into space of his beard is unbearably poignant."

This painting is by the same artist as the last one: a man with a rather slippery grasp of bodily form but with a sharp understanding of death.

Again, this is an extraordinary image. Jesus is painfully uncoordinated. It may be merely artistic ineptitude, but the unrealistic jutting into space of his beard is unbearably poignant. It is almost an abstraction of death. No corpse ever looked like this, but this may be how lifelessness needs to be seen. The body is all at odds with itself and the world around it, with the chest impossibly ribbed and the neck impossibly long. Indeed, the painting is rich in impossibilities that are strangely convincing. With his mother, Mary, John, and the two helpers are the other Marys, the three who are to come to the tomb on Sunday and find that the Lord is risen. They are carrying jars of ointment with which to anoint him, though this too will not happen for another three days.

It was only after the Resurrection that the guards were found asleep. In fact, there were no guards at first: Pilate stations them there only after protest from those who fear that the body may be stolen and resurrection pretended. (Despite the intense grief, there was clearly always a feeling that death for Jesus might not be final—and if his enemies so feared, what must his friends have hoped?)

Here the artist conflates life and death. Jesus is being buried, but time has been contracted so that the three Marys stand where they will be standing on Easter Sunday, vases of ointment at the ready, and the soldiers are seen in a condition of slumber. They are indeed only token soldiers, as they were to prove in reality. Only one of them has an actual face: the other two are disguised (not to say extinguished) by their hats, and all three convey a nice sense of waiting peacefully for the resurrection that is so obviously imminent. But it does not seem at all imminent when we look at Jesus's limp body, and it is this double vision—seeing how truly dead he is on one level, yet understanding how alive he is at a deeper level—that makes this picture so unforgettable. The painter has it both ways, and both are valid.

JESUS LAID IN THE TOMB
Anon., *The Office of the Blessed Virgin Mary*, Florence, 1420–30

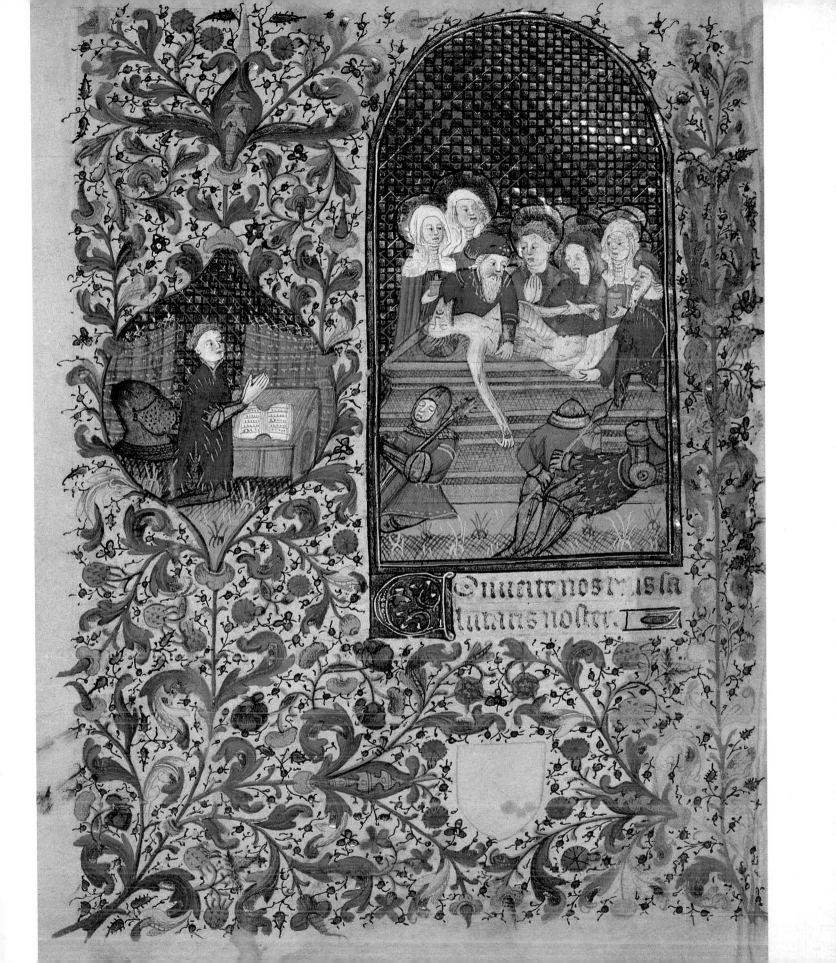

Onuutrnos i̇r isla
lutans nostit.

DEATH AND RESURRECTION

This striking, very early miniature has been published before. If it comes to us without surprise, it nevertheless comes with great impact: a most powerful summary of the climax of Christ's life, showing both his death and resurrection. Death looms large, occupying two-thirds of the page. All the events of the Passion are present here: the soldiers—a bored huddle at the foot of the cross—gambling for the garments of Jesus; to the right the three Marys—the grieving women who alone stayed faithful when all the others had fled—and to the left a resolute Mary and a shuddering Saint John. The thieves die in their different ways, one defiant to the end, one humbly repentant and receiving heavenly absolution. Jesus is respectfully clothed in a tunic, even though the artist knew full well that he would historically have been pitiably naked. But this artist was painting too near to the actual date to feel able to show his Lord in anything that seemed undignified. His Jesus is pale but in control: he does not allow death to overcome him, he is not its captive. Even his nailed feet seem free. To Jesus's right, with his name above, is the centurion who thrust a spear into his side to prove he was dead. Blood and water came out, says St John—Jesus had been totally drained of blood by then—and the centurion cried out: "Truly this man was the son of God."

The lower half of the picture explains the appearance of the crucified Jesus: he is also the risen Jesus. Here is the tomb, with its crumpled mass of sleeping guards, though one of them has "seen" and is in panicked flight. On the left are the women come to anoint the body. They find only an angel who tells them that Jesus has risen. (Immediately above the tomb, in the upper section, we see that "risen" Jesus, still hanging in death, but visibly master.) Finally, on the far right, Jesus encounters what we first think is Mary Magdalen and her companion. Yet the large halo looks strangely like that of Mary the Virgin, and it could be that this Byzantine icon maker sees that special Mary, the mother of Jesus, as the seeker on the left and the finder on the right, as well as the mourner above. We should never think of the death of Christ without recalling and rejoicing in his resurrection and here this is made visible.

THE CRUCIFIXION AND THE RESURRECTION
Anon., *Book of the Gospels in Syriac*,
Florence, 6th Century

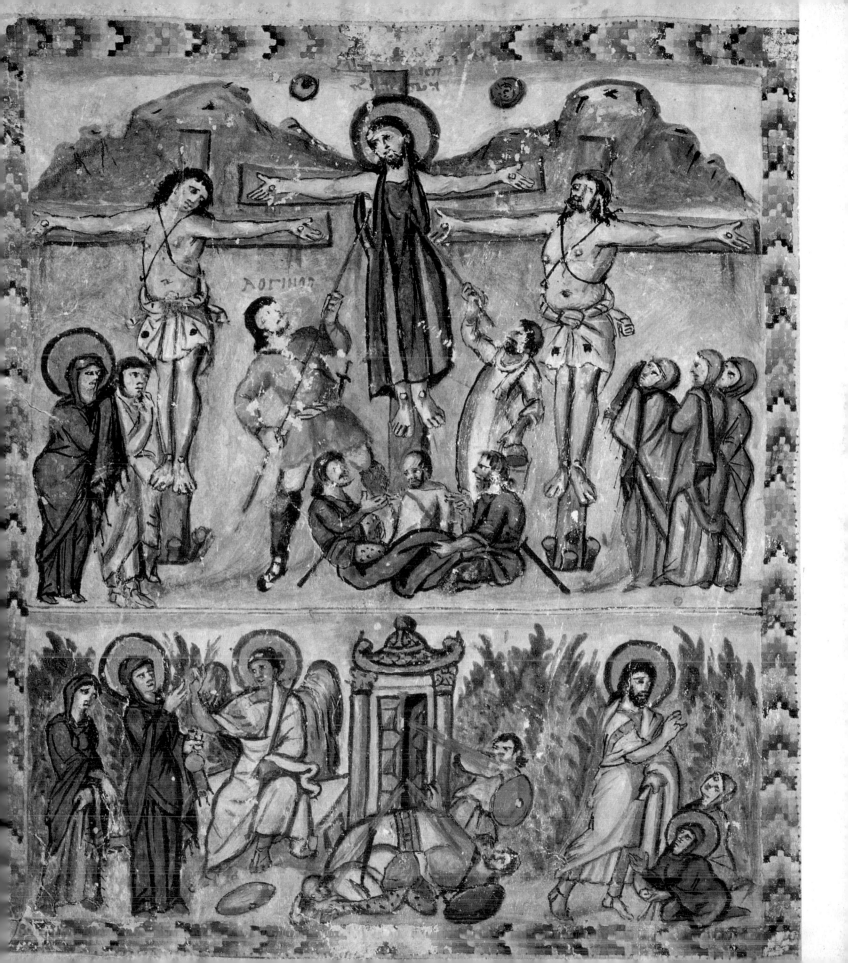

THE RESURRECTION

This is resurrection in all its clarity, with a tall, victorious Christ stepping in solemn majesty from his tomb, the long marble slab of its cover still propped up beside him. Squashed and inadequate, his guards sleep in their medieval chainmail, their useless spears pointing skywards and armorial shields dangling down. They are defended against any eventuality except the truth of Jesus, and the one exposed area of their body, the face, bears the silly smirk of that self-confidence that prevents the prejudiced from ever changing.

By rising from the dead, Jesus has, in fact, changed the world, but the world must accept it, and the crumpled faces below, hostile and stupid, suggest little hope. The last words of Jesus on the cross, Saint John tells us, were: "It is consummated." A vernacular translation might be: I have done it! Jesus must have died in an ecstasy of joy, knowing at last that he had completed the work that he was born to accomplish.

Jesus had defined his task as being that of listening to the Father, "doing always the things that please him." The Father's pleasure has always been that his sons and daughters should realize their own personal potential.

It was the work of Jesus to show by example and by teaching what it means to be truly human and to carry that through into death and beyond. His surrender to his Father was so total (remember, this is not mere man but God-made-man) that it carries us along with it. In Jesus we become what Adam was made to be—happy. It may be a painful happiness for us, who do not live in Paradise, but it is real to the extent that it is open to the truth. Glory gleams from this painting, with its exciting vigour and its directness of approach. "It is done," the bridge has been crossed. Now Jesus, our "pioneer" as the author of the Book of Hebrews calls him, steps forward to lead us. This is a wounded Jesus, the blood still clearly visible, but the wounds are no longer hurting. No pain is destructive unless we allow it to be so: even death itself can be transformed.

THE RESURRECTION
Anon., *Psalter,* Venice, 1270–80

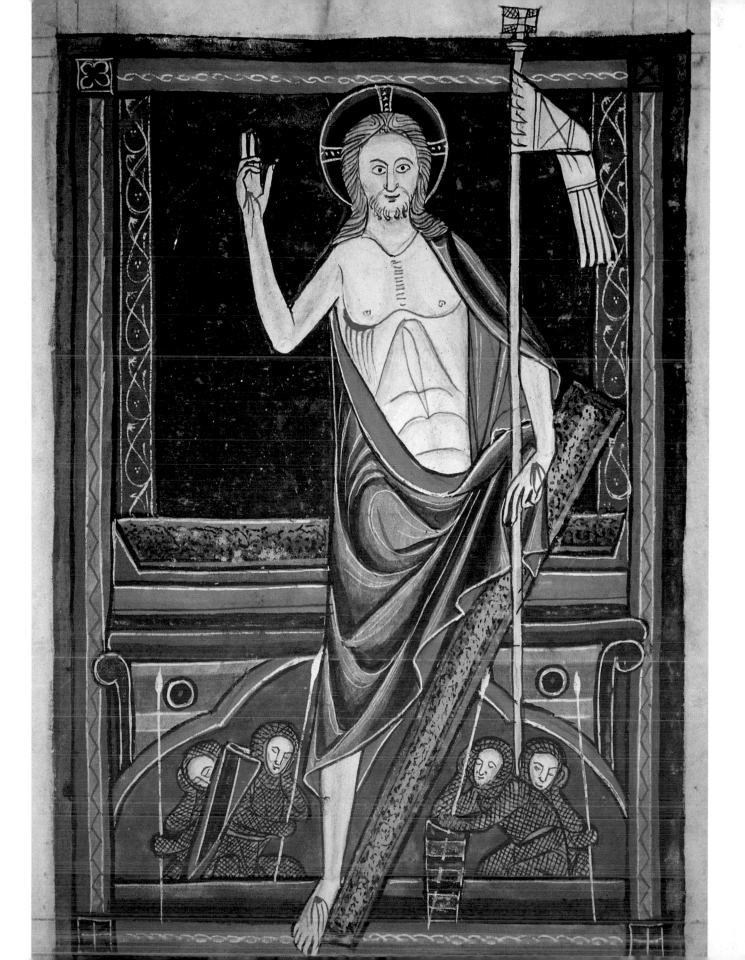

THE EMPTY TOMB

We know this is the empty tomb because it has "sepulcher" inscribed within, in small, pathetic script. The Marys are likewise named, standing before the tomb with their useless jars of embalming ointment. But this is only a notional tomb, far too small to contain a human body, and it brings to mind two other suggestions. One is that this oblong hollow, open at the top, even provided with what look uncommonly like feet, resembles a crib, the first bed of Jesus at his happy birth in the stable. Both at his birth and at his death, Christ's body was placed there by others, and neither structure was to hold his body for long.

But the other possible interpretation is even more convincing, since it may well rest on an historical truth. This tomb calls to mind a tabernacle, the small receptacle in which the consecrated bread lies, awaiting Communion time. Jesus in the form of bread is, supremely, the given Jesus, sacrificed for us and there for our taking. He had promised to be with us "always, until the very end of time," and in the

HOLY SATURDAY
The church celebrates Holy Saturday by exposing an empty tabernacle. The tabernacle is waiting to be filled with Eucharistic bread (representing the body of Christ) after the Resurrection Mass is celebrated.

tabernacle that promise is visibly true. Jesus belongs to all, he is "for us."

The artist who created this haunting picture will have seen that empty tabernacle, a silent witness, and may have reproduced it here. The Marys are bewildered, unable to cope with circumstances beyond their expectation. They draw no sensible deduction and derive no comfort from the empty tomb. Theirs appears to be a narrow faith, that can seek for Christ only in the accustomed places, whereas he wants to strengthen our trust by extending the possibilities for finding his presence.

THE EMPTY TOMB
Anon., *Concerning the Virginity of Mary,*
Florence, 10th Century

sepulcrum

mulier · annahu·

petrunca · uannicett ·

MARY MAGDALEN AT THE TOMB

The glory of this first miniature is Mary Magdalen's complete lack of interest in the angel sitting comfortably on the top of the tomb. One would expect so unusual a sight to arrest her attention, at the least. But nothing can deflect her from her desire for Jesus: even dead, he is still her heart's desire. We see her craning inelegantly forward, pathetically searching inside what is clearly an empty tomb. The angel looks benignly down, prepared to enter into helpful conversation, but Mary Magdalen is obsessed. So total is her determination to find the body and "take him away" that she does not register the figure moving in the middle distance. When she does see him, Scripture tells us that she thought he must be "the gardener."

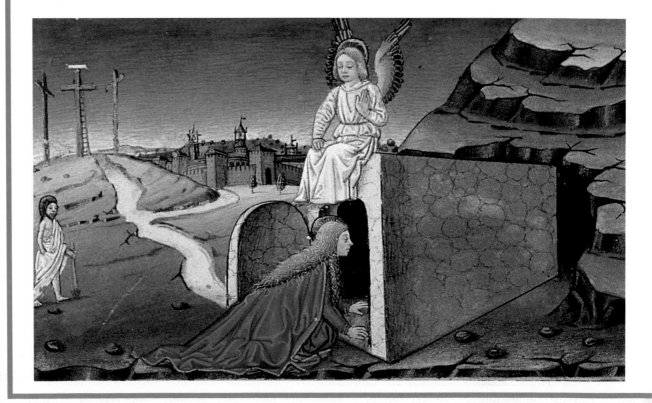

In the second miniature, she accosts him, weeping, begging for news about the new burial place. Only when "the gardener" addresses her by name; "Mary," do the scales fall from her eyes and she is free to recognize that she is speaking to Jesus himself.

It is a well-known story, how Mary Magdalen reaches out to Jesus, and how he tells her not to cling to him: *Noli me tangere*. He is not yet ascended, he adds, and there is work for her to do. Jesus wants her to hasten to the apostles, sunk in helpless sorrow in the Jerusalem we can see behind him, and tell them that he is risen. But what Mary wants to do is stay with her miraculously restored Lord, to gaze at him, to be silent in her overflowing joy. Put in a less dramatic way, she wants to pray. But prayer is a way of responding to God, and for her, prayer at this moment means activity. Jesus asks her to surrender the happiness of remaining in his presence, and instead to run into the noisy city, with messages that the apostles will find unconvincing. She was not at first believed: "women's tales," they said. Yet, as she had not found him in the beginning of the story, though he was there for the finding, so she does not make the same mistake again (Mary was a quick learner!). She had determined in advance that Jesus was in the tomb; she was wrong and nearly missed him. Now Mary is certain she needs time with him, but Jesus has to correct her again. She will "be with him" if she obeys and forgoes staying close to him. This time she understands.

left and below:
NOLI ME TANGERE
Cristoforo de Predis,
Concerning the Life of
Saint Joachim . . . ,
Turin, 1476

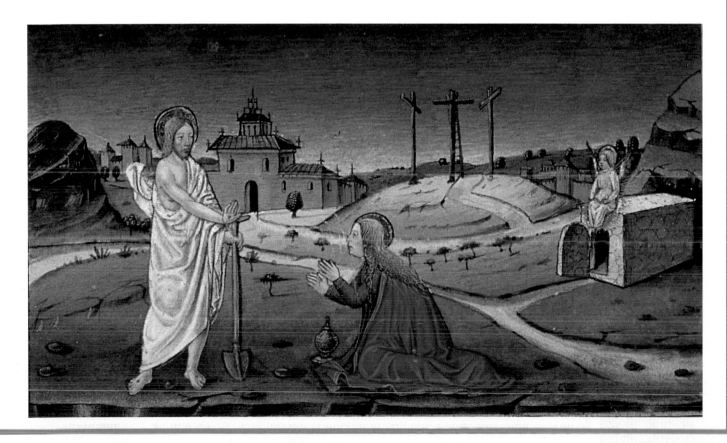

THE ASCENSION

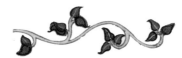

Christ stayed on earth, in a visible human form, for forty days after his resurrection. He did not suddenly disappear. Saint Mark tells us He impressed upon the disciples that they must go out into the world and preach the good news (the gospel) to every living creature, then, "the Lord Jesus was taken up into heaven and enthroned at the right hand of God."

In this painting the apostles crane upward, longing and yearning. Saint John, prominent as ever, seems utterly dismayed, while the others close their eyes in anguish and in reverence. Only Mary seems at peace. She knows for certain that Jesus has merely gone away in a bodily sense: he is present spiritually and always will be. What this painting emphasizes is that he really has departed from this world in a physical sense.

From now on, people will know him by faith alone; they will love him and understand his teaching, but without ever seeing him. Doubting Thomas—those may be his hands we can see raised in a forlorn attempt to stay the departure—said he could only believe if he saw and touched, if he actually put his hands into the wounds. Jesus granted his request, but added somberly: "You believe because you have seen me. Blessed are those who have not seen and yet believe."

Since the Ascension, we have all been among these actual or potential blessed ones. We shall never see Christ, and faith that demands sight is like faith that demands proof: there can be no true "belief" when there is evidence. The expression on all these faces is a poignant reminder of how dear Christ was to his friends and how much he would be missed. We may feel that we can never experience this natural emotional link with him, but our fate is in fact "more blessed": we have to choose to know him and thus discover for ourselves the happiness of his friendship.

The apostles, all of whom had spent years with Christ on the road, all left him and denied their faith: the Resurrection gave them their second chance—and God is the great giver of chances, one after the other. There is little advantage, it would seem, in having had this intimacy: we are equally privileged knowing him through prayer alone. Yet, when we look at these faces we cannot help wondering enviously what this human closeness must have been like.

THE ASCENSION
Simon Marmion, Gheraert Heronbout, Alexander Bening attrib., *The Blessed Virgin Mary's Book of Hours*, Naples, 1483–98

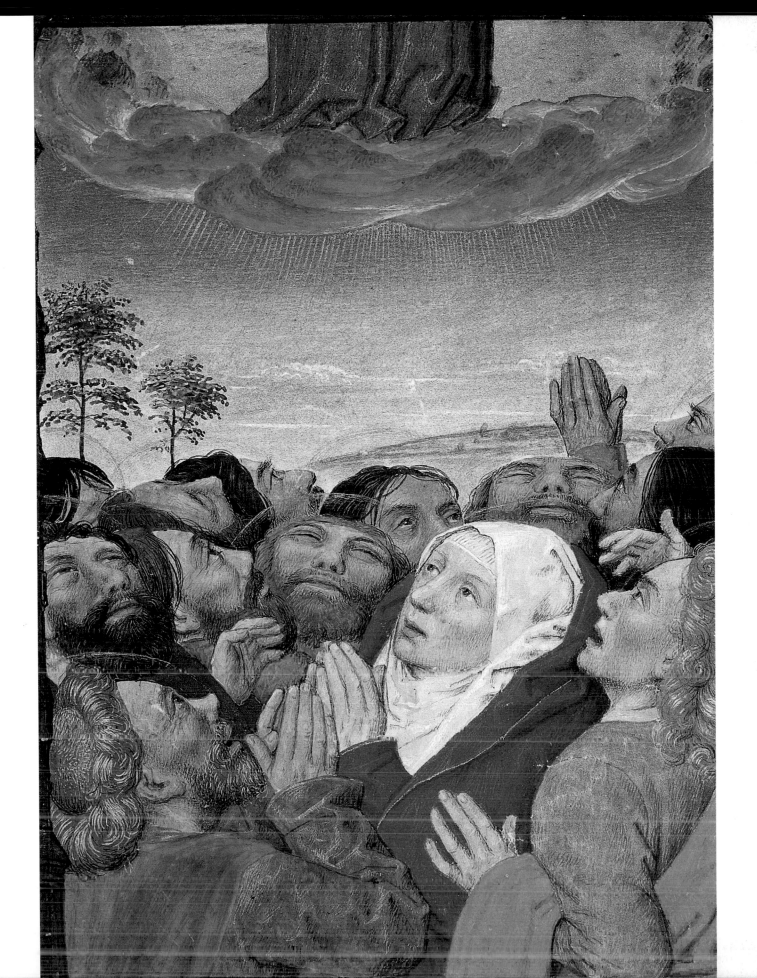

THE ASCENSION (II)

This artist is more into body language than facial expression. Mary and the apostles, with a forgiven Peter prominent on the right, indicate by their extravagant gesticulation that they will miss the physical presence of Jesus unbearably.

In the Acts of the Apostles, the sequel to his gospel, Saint Luke describes this Ascension scene, and how "they were still staring into the sky when two men in white were suddenly standing near them and said: Men of Galilee, why stand here looking into the sky?" The men, by implication, were angels, and the message is clear—we must not pine for what we cannot have, in this case, the sight of Jesus. The apostles were to go back to the city and set about the work Jesus had left them to complete.

The angels here are quite vehement, their brown wings reiterating the lesson of their eloquent fingers. Yet this artist does not show Jesus as having truly disappeared: He is still there, but now enclosed in a mandorla, that almond-shape used by the Greek Church to signify the holy. He holds the Bible in one hand and a rod in the other. Is this a shepherd's staff? Or the flag with which artists mark out the Resurrection? The apostles, we assume, cannot see him, yet he is there.

The point the artist seems to be making, however implicit, is that not having physical sight is unimportant. Once Jesus came into the world, and he has never left it. His presence pervades and transforms its atmosphere.

Two thousand years after his birth, we may not have grown appreciably closer to what we were meant to be, but we understand better.

There is no excuse now, not for ignorance nor despair. We are not asked to become holy, but to allow Jesus to make us holy, which is quite another matter. Unseen but all-powerful, Jesus is with us, everywhere. Every time we pray we are drawn into that mandorla, alone with him, and every time we act in love he is there with us. His preresurrection body could only be in one place at one time, and that body has now ascended: we are alive in the presence of the mystical body.

THE ASCENSION
Anon., *Book of the Gospels*, **Florence**
10th–11th Century

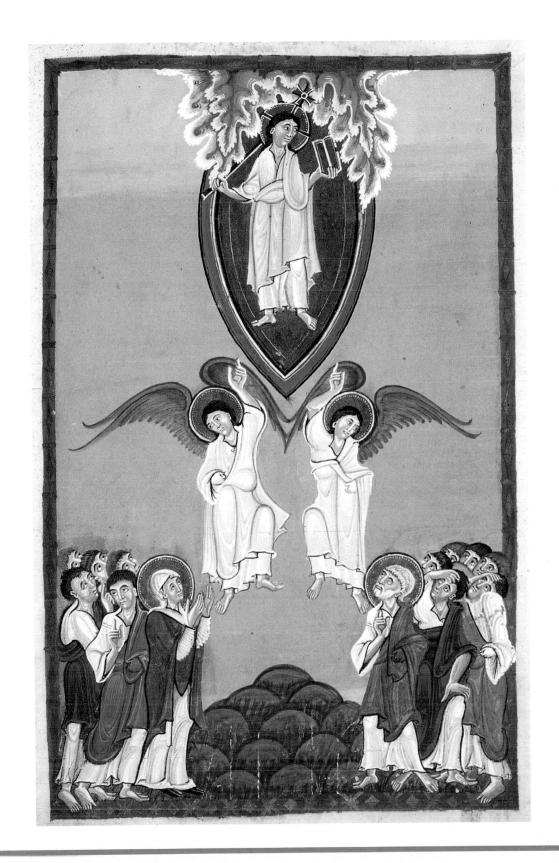

THE COMING OF THE HOLY SPIRIT

> *"Before he died, Jesus promised to send this Spirit ... and pledged to his friends that this Spirit would 'teach them,' at a depth greater than he could reach himself."*

The Spirit of Jesus, the third person of the Blessed Trinity, is the symbol that God's love is essentially outgoing.

The Father and the Son could make an exclusive pairing, loving each other and yet unfruitful. By telling us there is a mysterious "third," a presence who can only be described as the Holy Spirit, Jesus ensured that we would see God's love (to which ours aspires) as social, communal, all-embracing. Before he died, Jesus promised to send this Spirit, "the Spirit of Truth," and pledged to his friends that this Spirit would "teach them," at a depth greater than he could reach himself.

The Spirit teaches from within, and the sacrament of Confirmation, in which a Christian offers himself—or herself—to this Spirit is a crucial moment in a spiritual life.

In the Acts of the Apostles, Saint Luke speaks with awe of the coming of the Spirit, when Mary and the apostles were together in an upper room in Jerusalem. The house shook, as if a great gale were blowing, but the artist makes no attempt to portray this. Then "parted tongues, as it were of fire," descended and hovered over each head, and this is the moment shown here. We feel almost embarrassed, looking full into these faces that are receiving so stupendous a gift, the Holy Spirit. Every face is weighty with experience, eyes fixed, minds lost in the wonder of this heavenly communication. The symbolic dove wafts gently overhead. The experience, we are told, was transforming. The upper room had been chosen for their meeting because "of fear." The apostles were without courage—preaching the gospel seemed to them a shortcut to a death like that of the Lord. They were ashamed of their timidity, yet they were helpless to resist it.

The coming of the Holy Spirit changed them—he took away their fear, lit up their minds with the recollection of what Jesus had taught them, and gave them inner peace, joy, patience, and strength. He made them aware they had only to turn to Jesus and his Spirit was theirs for the asking. They could live in the strength and love of God. But here, that knowledge has not yet penetrated. The apostles are still in a state of holy shock.

THE PENTECOST
Anon., *The Office of the Blessed Virgin Mary's Book of Hours*, Turin, late 15th Century

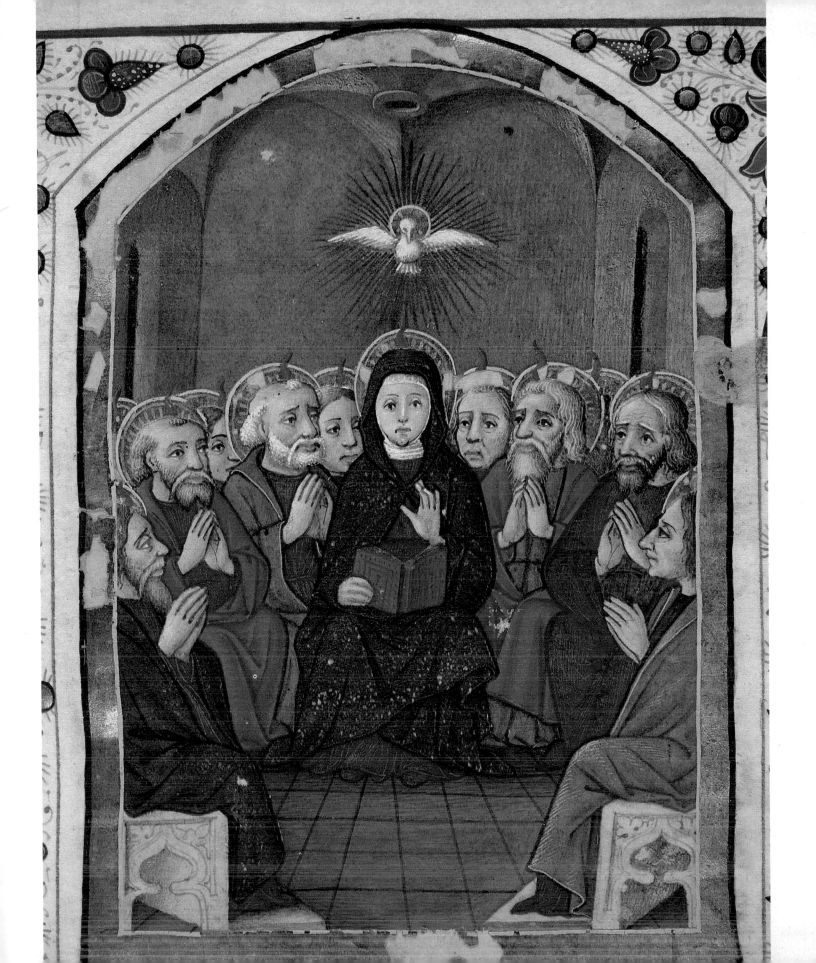

THE DEATH TO GLORY

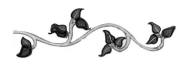

> "By his very coming, Jesus showed us something of God's love that we could never have imagined—but there was so much more to come after."

This illuminated page is a summary of the mysteries with which Christ's life ended, the end toward which he had steadfastly traveled since his birth. At the upper right is the Crucifixion, or rather its immediate consequence: the body of Jesus has been taken down and laid in the arms of his mother. It will be Saint John who crouches at the feet of the dead Jesus, but we remember earlier scenes, when it was Saint Joseph, loyal supporter, who stood by Mary as she caressed her child. That was a time of joy as intense as this is one of pain.

To the upper left is the sepulcher and the implicit resurrection. We see the empty tomb, the angel, gently explaining the wonder to the anxious women: could the news have seemed too good to be true? The useless guards huddle in a corner, a symbol of the powerlessness of worldly authority upon the Lord's followers. At the lower right, Mary, isolated, says farewell for a time to her son as he ascends into heaven; and, to the left, we see the grieving apostles swallowed up in radiance as Jesus sends down his Spirit upon them.

There is the sense of a Eucharistic meal here too, because it is in "the breaking of bread" that Jesus reveals himself and his Spirit is free to activate our hearts.

As paintings go, this one is not spectacular. There is more grace than power in the drawing and the colors are faded. Yet it is a beautiful and dignified compendium of the events that matter most to the followers of Jesus.

The Holy Birth was not only important in itself. By his very coming, Jesus showed us something of God's love that we could never have imagined—but there was so much more to come after.

The birth can seem all happiness, and so a birth should be. But we know from Saint Paul that Jesus "was like us in all things, sin alone excepted." He went through the difficulties of life, like us, and he changed defeat into victory. He took pain and rejection and made them redemptive, he entered into death accepting the Father's will and took away its horror forever. We know that in Jesus we shall pass through death and into bliss.

The message is still too momentous for us to take in, but we have the Holy Spirit to teach us and to make the impossible happen.

THE CRUCIFIXION TO GLORY
Anon., *Evangelarium,* **Parma, 11th Century**

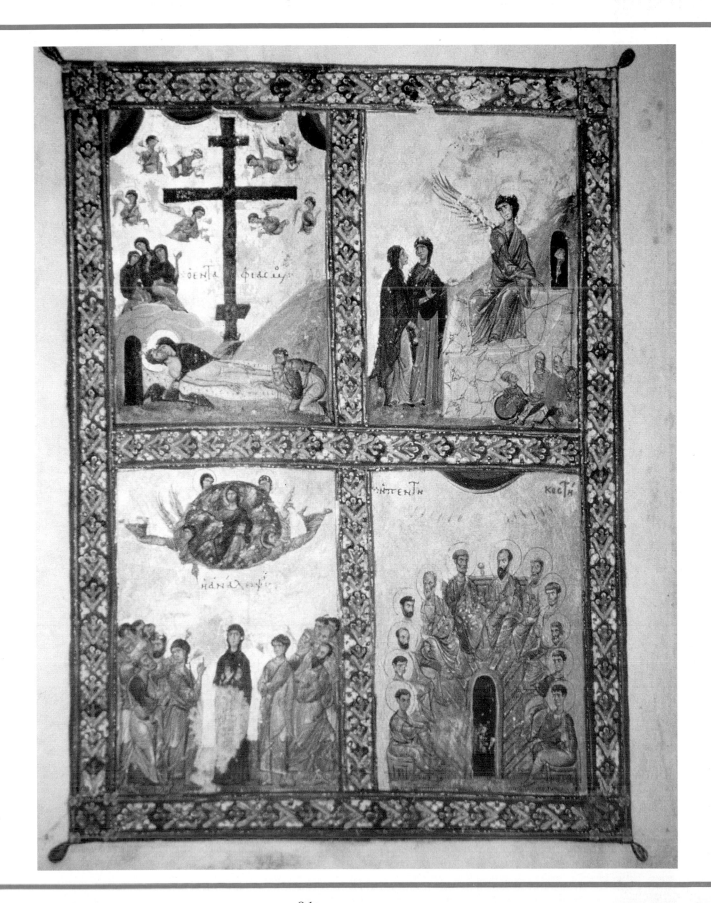

HEAVEN

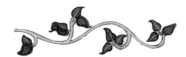

"Jesus came down from heaven to take us back with him. Whether we consciously accept this or not, it is so."

This is where the story ends, in heaven. It is not, here, a very wonderful heaven, since the artist is not a very wonderful artist, but we have it on the word of Jesus that "it has not entered the human heart to conceive what things God has prepared for those who love him." A token heaven is as good as we need, then, a reminder of where we shall all live eternally.

Heaven is a place where Jesus reigns, and that is all it requires by way of definition. He holds the orb of the world and raises his hand in benediction, wholly at rest, all pain and striving finally over. "It is consummated," his work is done. Mary sits in peace at his side, and his cousin, John the Baptist, who was called by him in Elizabeth's womb, sits on the other side.

Then the great throng of saints crowds in, with Michael the Archangel in the center and the kings and prophets of the Old Testament, as well as familiar friends from later on.

There is Peter (now a saint) clutching the keys of the church, bishops, a pope, a cardinal in his splendid red, soldiers, monks, nuns, Mary Magdalen with her jar of ointment, and Catherine with her wheel of martyrdom.

The artist makes it clear that this is only a cross-section: heaven is vast, he suggests, extending infinitely on either side. He has merely given us a window through which to look, remembering that one day we shall be here ourselves.

But, for now, this is a picture of heaven set in an earthly frame. Birds and flowers surround it, and beneath, to keep us alert, there is the menace of the dragon. It attacks only those who give way to their own inner dragon, the lascivious and the flippant, and all those who do not take responsibility to heart.

We, like Jesus, were born for heaven; it is, as scripture finely puts it, "our homeland." Our awareness of this explains the perpetual appeal of the gospel story, from birth to death and into life again. Jesus came down from heaven to take us back with him. Whether we consciously accept this or not, it is so. And so it will be.

GLORIA
Anon., *The Blessed Virgin Mary's Book of Hours*, **Turin, 15th Century**

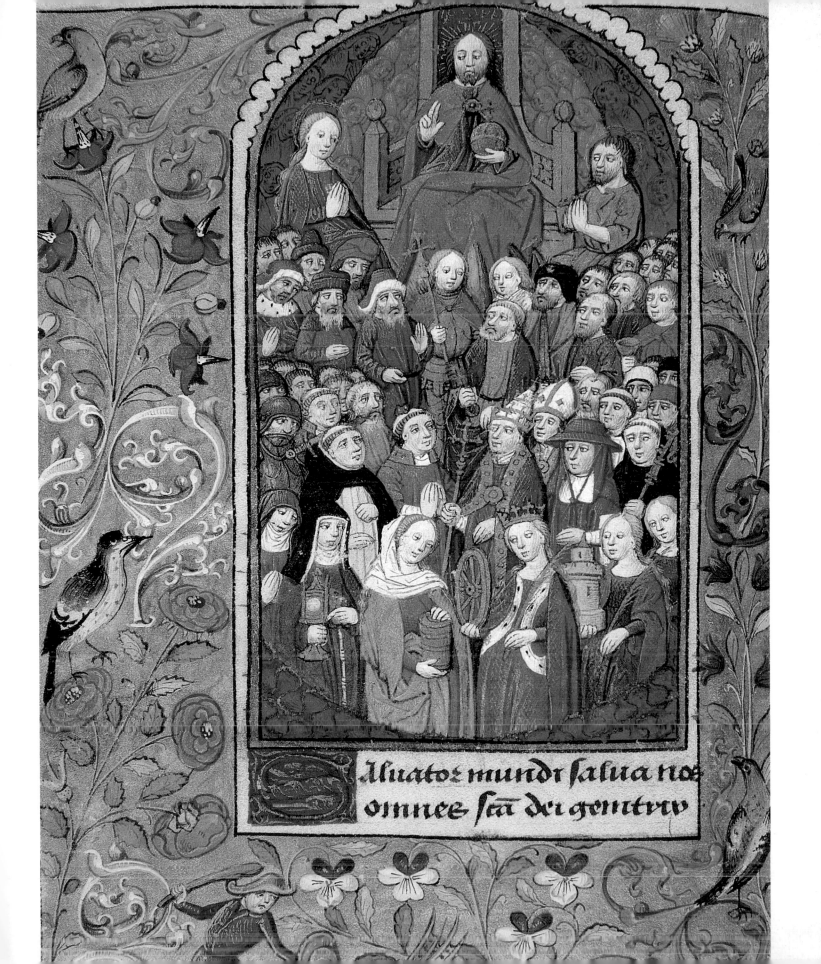

INDEX

PICTURE SOURCES

HarperCollins*Publishers* and Rose Publishing would like to thank the following for their kind permission to reproduce images:

FLORENCE:

BIBLIOTECA MEDICEA LAURENZIANA (THE MEDICI LIBRARY)
PAGE 15 Conv. Soppr. 582 c1r, *Biblia*, Bible 318x214mm
PAGES 16,17,19 Edili 125 c5v, *Biblia*, Bible 575x395mm
PAGE 31 Ashb. 17 c67r, *De virginitate Sanctae Mariae*, Concerning the Virginity of Mary, 215x159mm
PAGE 77 Plut I,56 c13v, *Evangelarium*, Book of the Gospels in Syriac, 335x225mm
PAGE 81 Ashb. 17 c57r, *De virginitate Sanctae Mariae*, Concerning the Virginity of Mary, 215x159mm
PAGE 87 Acq. e Doni 91 c96r, *Evangelarium*, Book of the Gospels, 355x254mm

BIBLIOTECA RICCARDIANA (THE RICCARDI LIBRARY)
PAGE 25 Ricc 466 c29r, *Officium Beatae Mariae Virginis*, The Office of the Blessed Virgin Mary, 120x87mm
PAGE 29 Ricc 456 c37v, *Officium Beatae Mariae Virginis*, The Office of the Blessed Virgin Mary, 158x112mm
PAGE 41 Ricc 323 c14v, *Psalterium*, Psalter, 220x160mm
PAGE 65 Ricc 429 c170r, *Officium Beatae Mariae Virginis*, The Office of the Blessed Virgin Mary, 215x140mm
PAGE 73 Ricc 429 c178r, *Officium Beatae Mariae Virginis*, The Office of the Blessed Virgin Mary, 215x140mm
PAGE 75 Ricc 429 c179v, *Officium Beatae Mariae Virginis*, The Office of the Blessed Virgin Mary, 215x140mm

MODENA:

BIBLIOTECA ESTENSE E UNIVERSITARIA (THE ESTENSE AND UNIVERSITY LIBRARY)
PAGE 39 Lat 842= alfa.R.7.3 c14v, *Officium Beatae Mariae Virginis*, The Office of the Blessed Virgin Mary, 222x156mm
PAGE 63 Lat 842= alfa.R.7.3 c166r, *Officium Beatae Mariae Virginis*, The Office of the Blessed Virgin Mary, 222x156mm

NAPLES:

BIBLIOTECA NAZIONALE 'VITTORIO EMANUELE III' (THE 'VICTOR EMANUEL III' NATIONAL LIBRARY)
PAGE 21 I B 53 c12v, *Horae Beatae Mariae Virginis kum Kalendario*, The Blessed Virgin Mary's Book of Hours with Calendar, 253x140mm
PAGE 27 I B 27 c43r, *Horae Beatae Mariae Virginis secundum usum rothomagensis ecclesiae*, The Blessed Virgin Mary's Book of Hours According to the Usage of the Church of Rouen, 258x180mm
PAGE 43 I B 27 c85r, *Horae Beatae Mariae Virginis secundum usum rothomagensis ecclesiae*, The Blessed Virgin Mary's Book of Hours According to the Usage of the Church of Rouen, 258x180mm
PAGE 69 I B 51 c59v, *Horae Beatae Mariae Virginis cum Kalendario—detto "La Flora,"* The Blessed Virgin Mary's Book of Hours with Calendar—known as "La Flora," 204x134mm
PAGE 85 I B 51 c253v, *Horae Beatae Mariae Virginis cum Kalendario—detto "La Flora,"* The Blessed Virgin Mary's Book of Hours with Calendar—known as "La Flora," 204x134mm

PARMA:

BIBLIOTECA PALATINA (THE PALATINE LIBRARY)
PAGE 91 Palat. 5 c90v, *Evangelarium*, Book of the Gospels in Greek, 300x231mm

TURIN:

BIBLIOTECA REALE (THE ROYAL LIBRARY)
PAGE 35 Varia 77 c16r, *Officium Beatae Mariae Virginis*, The Office of the Blessed Virgin Mary, 195x135mm
PAGE 45 Varia 77 c18v, *Officium Beatae Mariae Virginis*, The Office of the Blessed Virgin Mary, 195x135mm
PAGE 47 Varia 78 c60r, *Officium Horae Beatae Mariae Virginis*, The Office of the Blessed Virgin Mary's Book of Hours, 190x140mm
PAGE 49 Varia 124 c41v, *Vita de santo Yoachin, e de santa Anna e de la nativitate de santa Maria e de lo nostro signior...*, Concerning the Life of Saint Joachim and Saint Anne and the births of the Blessed Virgin and of Our Lord..., 264x182mm
PAGE 53 Varia 88 c48r, *Horae Mariae Virginis cum Kalendario*, The Blessed Virgin Mary's Book of Hours with Calendar, 133x195mm
PAGE 56–7 Varia 124 cc90r-v, *Vita de santo Yoachin, e de santa Anna e de la nativitate de santa Maria e de lo nostro signior...*, Concerning the Life of Saint Joachim and Saint Anne and the births of the Blessed Virgin and of Our Lord..., 264x182mm
PAGE 58–9 Varia 124 cc65r-v, *Vita de santo Yoachin, e de santa Anna e de la nativitate de santa Maria e de lo nostro signior...*, Concerning the Life of Saint Joachim and Saint Anne and the births of the Blessed Virgin and of Our Lord..., 264x182mm
PAGE 67 Varia 124 c108v, *Vita de santo Yoachin, e de santa Anna e de la nativitate de santa Maria e de lo nostro signior...*, Concerning the Life of Saint Joachim and Saint Anne and the births of the Blessed Virgin and of Our Lord..., 264x182mm
PAGES 82-3 Varia 124 c127v, *Vita de santo Yoachin, e de santa Anna e de la nativitate de santa Maria e de lo nostro signior...*, Concerning the life of Saint Joachim and Saint Anne and the births of the Blessed Virgin and of Our Lord..., 264x182mm
PAGE 89 Varia 78 c17r, *Officium Horae Beatae Mariae Virginis*, The Office of the Blessed Virgin Mary's Book of Hours, 190x140mm
PAGE 93 Varia 88 c145v, *Horae Beatae Mariae Virginis cum Kalendario*, The Blessed Virgin Mary's Book of Hours with Calendar, 133x95mm

VENICE:

BIBLIOTECA NAZIONALE MARCIANA (ST MARK'S LIBRARY)
PAGE 8 Lat I,100 (=2089), *legatura*, bookcover, 290x210mm
PAGE 23 Lat I,77 (=2397) c13v, *Psalterium*, Psalter, 250x170mm
PAGE 37 Lat I,77 (=2397) c15v, *Psalterium*, Psalter, 250x170mm
PAGE 55 Lat I,77 (=2397) c20r, *Psalterium*, Psalter, 250x170mm
PAGE 79 Lat I,77 (=2397) c24r, *Psalterium*, Psalter, 250x170mm

VATICAN CITY:

BIBLIOTECA APOSTOLICA VATICANA (THE VATICAN'S APOSTOLIC LIBRARY)
PAGE 7 Barb. Lat 613 c514r, *Biblia di Niccolò III d'Este*, Bible of Niccolò III d'Este, 382x266mm
PAGE 61 Barb. Lat 610 c185r, *Messale per il battistero di Firenze*, Missal for the Baptistery in Florence, 390x290mm